More praise for *Loaves, Fishes, a*

"This is how theology ought to be done: in the lively exchange between people engaging life's most fundamental questions. Ted Loder's astute mind, pragmatic eloquence, and compassionate heart enable him to challenge, clarify, and comfort all at once. Here is wisdom, prophetic challenge, and theological clarity gleamed from five decades as a pastor, parent, spouse, and citizen who has been willing to engage, when necessary, in a lover's quarrel with his church and country. Ted Loder offers the rare gift of fresh perspectives on theological questions and timeless truths."

>—Julie Neraas, ordained Presbyterian clergywoman, spiritual director, and professor in the Graduate Liberal Studies Program, Hamline University

"A much-needed response to the conservative pull of American religious culture today . . . a lively, informative glimpse into the thought and faith of a liberal pastoral theologian."

>—Joan Hemenway, D.Min., retired pastoral educator and author

"In this refreshing approach to communication, Ted Loder exhibits the exemplary traits of the pastoral theologian: candor, attentiveness, a searching intelligence, and faithful—but not unquestioning—affirmation of the gospel. It is a tribute to him that these earnest seekers of his congregation have entrusted to him their most critical questions of life and faith. Both the questions and Ted's commentary represent practical theological dialogue at its best."

>—James L. Waits, President Emeritus, The Fund for Theological Education; former Executive Director, The Association of Theological Schools in the United States and Canada

Other books by Ted Loder:

Guerrillas of Grace:
Prayers for the Battle

The Haunt of Grace:
Responses to the Mystery of God's Presence

My Heart in My Mouth:
Prayers for Our Lives

Tracks in the Straw:
Tales Spun from the Manger

Wrestling the Light:
Ache and Awe in the Human/Divine Struggle

Loaves, Fishes, and Leftovers

Sharing Faith's Deep Questions

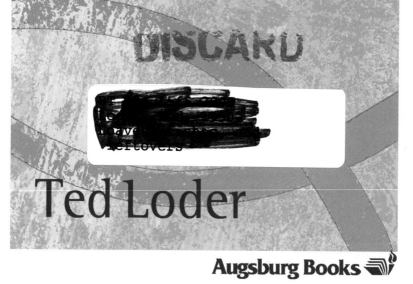

Ted Loder

Augsburg Books

MINNEAPOLIS

To William Sloane Coffin,
my beloved friend, colleague, and mentor,
with enormous gratitude and respect.

LOAVES, FISHES, AND LEFTOVERS
Sharing Faith's Deep Questions

Large-quantity purchases or custom editions of this book are available at a discount from the publisher. For more information, contact the sales department at Augsburg Fortress, Publishers, 1-800-328-4648, or write to: Sales Director, Augsburg Fortress, Publishers, P. O. Box 1209, Minneapolis, MN 55440-1209.

Scripture quotations are from the *New Revised Standard Version Bible*, copyright © 1989 by the Division of Christian Education of the National Council of the Churches of Christ in the USA. Used by permission.

"Loaves and Fishes" from the *House of Belonging*, copyright © 1997 by David Whyte. Used by permission of the author and Many Rivers Press. (www.davidwhyte.com)

ISBN 0-8066-5141-5

Cover design by Marti Naughton; cover art from Stephanie Dalton Cowan/ Artville/Symbols and Icons CD
Book design by Michelle L. N. Cook

The paper used in this publication meets the minimum requirements of American National Standard for Information Sciences—Permanence of Paper for Printed Library Materials, ANSI Z329.48-1984.♾™

Manufactured in the U.S.A.

09   08   07   06   05   1   2   3   4   5   6   7   8   9   10

"Loaves and Fishes"

This is not
the age of information.

This is *not*
the age of information.

Forget the news,
and the radio,
and the blurred screen.

This is the time
of loaves
and fishes.

People are hungry,
and one good word is bread
for a thousand.

–David Whyte

Contents

Acknowledgments | 9

Preface | 11

First Sharing | 13

hope and despair • participation in God's kingdom • morality and connections • God defines love • finding God • impact of small changes • prayer • anger at God • God as parent • relating to God • power of words • uncertainty, freedom, and faith • elements of religious authority • emergence of Scripture • Scripture and meaning • religion and secular world • anger and grief • God and human responsibility

Second Sharing | 38

Jesus' crucifixion and resurrection • communion • God and suffering • sin vs. sins • repentance • sin as ME-ism • facing pretensions • therapy and religion • freedom • fea • courage and trust • salvation as a dynamic process • God's ongoing resurrections • God's judgment • God's relation to Jesus • God's revelation in Jesus • God's plan vs. God's purpose • atonement • resurrection of the body • on-going-ness of relationships • what we're called to do • what's enough

Third Sharing | 71

Christianity and Civil Rights Movement • religion's impact on society • mission of church • church and homosexuality • conventional wisdom vs. morality • gay marriage • church/state and marriage • "Christian nation" • religion and the Pledge of Allegiance • marriage as covenant • divorce • morals and absolutes • covenant and God • "one or ninety-nine" • God's freedom • humility • shaky faith on a firm foundation • living in the mess • broken hearts and God's grace

Fourth Sharing / 96

grief for a soldier • Jesus and resurrection of body • life after death • personal continuity through time • heaven • resurrection key to Christianity • Jesus in Gospels • credibility of Gospels • Pentecost • Jesus and war • personal morality and political power • God and Caesar • pacifism • lover's quarrel with our country • centrality of Jesus • assurance vs. certainty • Coffin's prophetic voice • Christian realism • confronting controversial issues • kingdom of God among us

Fifth Sharing / 124

ethics of conviction • Christianity's continuing reformation • H. Richard Niebuhr's definition of God • a Christlike God • involvement in religious conflicts • loving enemies • conscientious objectors • response to war • love of God and neighbor • worth of humans • true self-interest • reconciliation with others • moral decision making • reconciliation with God • human longing • risks of love • inner warfare • persistence of hope • claims of justice • Pro-Life/Pro-Choice • faith and dialogue

Sixth Sharing / 155

evil • Devil/Satan • temptation • demons • God and evil · beauty • creativity • what's right with the world • science and religion • God as improviser • Theory of Emergence • God's plan vs. God's purpose, revisited • faithfulness to God • calling and career • importance of individual action • validity of prayers of petition • prayer as teacher • death as teacher • stepping into mystery • healing • prayers for others • answers to prayers • personal story • being believable

Acknowledgments

I am deeply grateful for the honesty, integrity, and fidelity of the persons who contributed so generously and substantially to *Loaves, Fishes, and Leftovers* through the question and answer sessions we shared.

Marcia Broucek, book editor and former publisher
Amy Allison D'Ancona, parent; Philadelphia high school English teacher
Emily D'Ancona, graduate student in elementary education
Gretel C. DeRuiter, middle school English teacher
Ann Marie Donohue, Ph.D., psychologist and college faculty member
Stephen Duffy, upper school principal
Janet I. Filing, Ph.D., teacher and family therapist
Edith Giese, former executive director, National Gray Panthers
Ernest R. Giese, teacher of deaf and hard-of-hearing, retired
Bill Harrington, advisor to microfinance organizations in developing countries
Joanne Jack, fifth grade teacher
Emily Jack-Scott, student at Yale University
Susan L. Jensen, organizing consultant
Richard C. Josiassen, Ph.D., clinical neuroscientist
Rita Shaughnessy Josiassen, M.D., Ph.D., psychiatrist in academic setting
Karen Loder, Ted's daughter and friend; parent; independent school development director
Carl McHenry, electrical engineer, project manager
Roberta Millard, teacher of high school English and media studies
Elesa Nelson, high school guidance counselor
Michael Taras, student at University of Vermont
Joe Waldo, sales and marketing professional
Rosemary Walkenhorst, paralegal and office manager
Ted Walkenhorst, attorney representing the disabled

Preface

Not all ideas turn out to be good, but this one did. Why not take a Sunday and replace the sermon with an opportunity for people to ask questions to which I would respond spontaneously? At first it felt risky but exciting. I tried it, and the congregation, tentative at first, became excited about it as well. That was the beginning of devoting two worship occasions a year to that format. I called these experiments "question and answer sermons." That was wrong on two counts. They weren't sermons, and my responses were not answers—at least in the sense of being complete or conclusive. Rather they expressed my theological education and thinking, as well as my experience as a Christian and a pastor. The excitement was in the immediacy and relevance of what we shared to the vital issues with which people were wrestling. Of course, dialogue is assumed in writing and delivering sermons, but in these instances it was publicly expressed by the interchange between us.

The questions consistently revealed the faith struggles of the questioner and most others in the congregation. In a sense they were my questions as well. It was a mutual exploration and a reminder that such mutuality is the process that pertains to all Christian life. The openness and intensity of those Sunday sessions stretched our understanding not only of worship but also of faith and life itself. They provided a deeper context and spirit for ongoing dialogue in and out of church. People began asking variations of the questions more freely in other contexts: counseling, administrative meetings, mission projects, pastoral visits, even in community events.

It wasn't until I'd retired from the formal pastorate and a small group asked if we could continue the Q&A format in someone's home that it dawned on me that maybe the most authentic metaphor for this process is the story of Jesus feeding the multitude. According to all four Gospels, about five thousand people gathered, listened to Jesus, and at the end of the day were hungry. Jesus asked the disciples to see what resources the people had. All they came up with were five loaves and two fish. Jesus took them, broke them into pieces, and when the crowd had eaten, there were twelve baskets of leftovers. I think that's a metaphor for the dialogical process of faith.

We gather, offer the loaves and fishes of our lives' experiences and mysteries, and there is always enough food and leftovers for us to keep going and growing in faith.

Loaves, Fishes, and Leftovers, compiled from transcripts of audio tapes of our small group sessions, reflects the ongoing human explorations of faith's deep questions. I offer *Loaves, Fishes, and Leftovers* as a testament of the recurring mystery of sharing, being blessed, fed, and strengthened to move on into ever deeper life, love, and trust in God.

First Sharing

Q: Let me begin with a question that's been on my mind a lot these days, and probably is on the minds of many others, too. What do you do when you feel that, everywhere you look, the world is going to hell in a hand basket? How do you not just look around and say, "Where's the hope?"

A: Well, the opposite of hope is despair. It's easy to despair. I despair two or three times a week. I think the deliverance from despair is to root ourselves in a bigger world view than the one in which most of us usually operate. We work and take care of our families. We have a social life and are citizens of the community and nation. We follow the news of the day. The trouble comes when we get bogged down in all that and forget that there is a larger, undergirding dimension to life.

I have to keep reminding myself that when we look at the world in the short view, we make God a liar. But when we take the long view, we can see the work of God unfolding to its purpose. I think that's a helpful reminder, especially if we allow that the long view is much longer than just our lifetime. To take the long view is to see that we are part of the purpose of life. This enables us to shift from passively hoping in the future to actively hoping the future in. That is to lay claim, in faith, that we are part of the kingdom of God even now.

Biblical scholar Walter Brueggemann says that essentially Scripture tells us four things: 1) God made us, 2) in love, 3) for a purpose, and 4) God works in our lives and the world to accomplish that purpose, one way or another, almost certainly in surprising ways. As Christians, we see that in Jesus' life and death and resurrection. That's where our hope is rooted.

Q: But staying rooted there is really hard. At least for me. I get beaten down.

A: A lot of people who care about the world share that experience. We can't hide from awful things unless we have Ph.D.s in denial, or see despair as a sign of sophistication somehow. You asked what to do when you feel the world is going to hell in a hand basket. The answer is in your question: What we *DO* is the key to the whole thing.

What we do first is pray. And among other things, we pray, "Thy Kingdom come, Thy will be done on earth as it is in heaven." Then we add, hopefully, "Let your kingdom come, your will be done through me, by me, in me, for me." After praying that, we try to *do* that prayer as best we can in our day-by-day world. Then we have to trust, which involves letting go at least a little of the outcome of our efforts, the supposed success or failure of them, and leaving the results to God. That can make us less afraid and less despairing. Because ultimately the kingdom is God's gift, not our achievement.

Q: Doesn't that contradict what you said about praying for God to let the kingdom come through us, or by us?

A: I don't think so. I believe *our* choice is whether we want to participate in God's kingdom by trying to live differently in the decisions and directions of every day. Not big decisions that are going to dramatically change the world. Those aren't given to most of us, to anyone really. That isn't reason to discount the value of the decisions that are ours to make. Like how we include and love and be just to those in our families, to our neighbors and enemies wherever they are—down the street, in the workplace, in our cities and suburbs, our state and nation, everywhere in our world. How we use our time and, that touchy subject, our money—what we give it to and for, the what and why of our political actions. In a word, how we hope the future in. Those are the "to do" things when we feel despairing.

But I have to add that to do those things, we need to be connected to others because we can't do them well or alone. You may have heard that old saying that tyrants are never more secure than when their victims are most isolated. Well, there's a subtle tyranny in reducing every part of life, even religion, to the individual, the individual's effort, and the individual's reward. In that process the social contract gets frayed, community unravels, and any sense of responsibility for the lives and good of others in the human family dissipates. So we get isolated. Privatization gets more entrenched and becomes the American dream, if not close to being religious doctrine, as though our faith is only about God, not about neighbor.

Unfortunately, the church's role in this process is sometimes one of collusion. I think in some crucial ways, the church has sold out to the values of success, institutional preservation, and avoidance of critical issues that might be controversial in the public areas and yet really matter in our personal lives. But when morality gets reduced to only personal morality, it becomes immoral. Jesus said, in Matthew 25, that it isn't just individuals but nations who are judged for what they do, or don't do, "for the least of these . . . ." When we privatize our faith, we don't feel or see ourselves as capable and responsible. Instead, we feel powerless and slip into despair. In our time, Good Samaritans need to be organized.

Q: Maybe that's why I feel more hopeful in this group.

A: I think probably we all do. When we're isolated, we lack nourishment, so to speak. We start complaining and blaming other people, and, on the other hand, nobody holds us accountable for our actions, omissions, and biases. Nobody confronts us and says, "Wait a minute, what about this?" Having our feet held to the fire pulls us out of the maze of self-preoccupation and sulking. We realize that there are others out there working, risking, caring, thinking, hoping, trusting, too.

What wearies me is the piety that keeps saying "God is love," which often ends up as a vaporous pretension that "love is God." Maybe I'm being too hard-nosed, but I really don't want to hear that anymore. It's too passive to fit God. It results in the misplaced assumption in that whenever we have love-y feelings, we're experiencing God—and when we don't have those feelings, God isn't around.

But if we grasp that God *defines* love, that turns things around. If we want to see God's love, look at Jesus. His life, teaching, and action are where God most clearly defines love for us. As Christians, we need to explore together what that love means and how it relates to us and our world. The mission of the church is to promote that process because it's at the core of the gospel.

Q: But people look to other places to find God. Or what love means. Are you saying that Jesus is the only place where we can find God?

A: Of course, people rightly can and do look other places to find God. God is *more* than we see in Jesus. But that isn't to say that God is *other* than what we see in Jesus, or that there's something about God that actually contradicts what we see in Jesus. For example, Jesus lived in a pre-scientific time so he would have seen the universe differently. And yet the real point is that he essentially understood it as God's creation, just as we believe that about the mystery of the universe.

It is God's world, so, yes, look to Abraham and Moses and the prophets; to other world religions; also to science, literature, the arts, psychology, philosophy. Nevertheless, for Christians Jesus is the primary place to see how God works in the world. Uniquely in Jesus we see, if only in a mirror dimly, something essential of what God's kingdom is about.

So what do we do when we feel the world is going to hell in a hand basket? We try live out God's love as we see it in Jesus and find other people who seriously try to do that as well. A community of faith and action makes the difference between hope and despair. Because hope is contagious, we catch it when we connect with others who gather in and act out of hope, who explore what it means to love sacrificially in this world.

Surely Christ's church ought, and sometimes is, the place where that connection and exploration happens. But it isn't the only place. God works in other "non-religious" ways, causes, and organizations, too. You've no doubt found some. To connect with such groups where we see God is working in the world hoists our sails to the winds of love and hope.

Q: Yes, but nothing much seems to change because of that. That's sort of the original question.

A: It may seem that not much changes, at least not very discernibly and probably not in our lifetime.

And yet who really knows but God? But, in fact, a lot of little changes take place before there's a big change. It's because of those little, often unnoticed, changes that a larger, more obvious change happens. That's my experience. I passionately believe that hope not only kick starts us into action but is leaven in the lump of time and the world.

And yet, I know where you're coming from. It does seem that the amount of good we do in the world is small compared with the enormity of the universe and snarled problems that plague us. But I believe what we do does add some fuel to the agitation of the kingdom in our midst, helps it lurch inch by inch toward becoming more real on earth. What we do makes a difference. It's like the miracle of the loaves and the fishes: God multiplies our little gifts to a great purpose beyond our wildest imagination. That's why I keep saying, and not really facetiously, that God is sneaky.

Q: You started talking about prayer a few minutes ago. I have trouble praying. At least in an organized way. Or sometimes at all. Do you schedule prayer time? What are your views about prayer?

A: This is a huge subject, isn't it? Let me begin by saying that for me, the core questions of prayer are *what* prayer is and *why* pray and to *whom*, not so much where, when, and how to pray. There are a lot of valid ways and forms of prayer. But they all have to do with becoming aware of and affirming that God's presence is the context in which we live every tick and twitch of our lives. They all relate to the awareness that what tousles our hair on the way to the car, or looks back at us in the eyes of another person, or makes us laugh, or cry, or wonder, or shiver at the stars, is a Presence who is more than we realize and makes life worth more than we know. That's the root of what prayer is about for me.

Q: That helps. But I still wonder what your prayer life is like.

A: Well, a regularly scheduled devotional period every day doesn't work too well for me, though I've kept at it periodically over the years. But somehow it doesn't work for me as it does for lots of others. It feels contrived and my mind starts to wander. So I've started praying about the things it wanders to because those things crowd in and press for my attention—which means my prayers. That's one form the discipline of prayer takes for me even if for some it lacks "discipline." Another discipline for me is writing prayers, pushing my way into deep praying that way.

Everyone needs to find their own way of praying, one that fits them and involves their mind and heart. Find it, then do it. Me? I pray all the time, not just some "time." I pray many, many times day, in all kinds of situations. Some prayers are longer than others. Rather than set a definite time apart to pray, I take prayer into all the hours of my day. And night, too, before I sleep or when I can't sleep or wake in the night.

Maybe it's God who wakes me, like Samuel when God called to him.[1]

The point is, it's important for me to have a reference outside of myself that I reach toward and try to include in what I do, and the way I do it, and why. Whether I'm thinking, reading, listening, speaking, being quiet and reflecting, deciding, or taking some action, being aware even dimly of that Other, that Presence, is what prayer is about for me—and all those ways are forms of prayer for me.

Q: Is your prayer, then, just about awareness? You don't pray for anything specific?

A: No, awareness is not all my prayers are about. They are very specific. Ann Lamott, in her terrific book *Traveling Mercies*, says her most used prayers are "Thank you, thank you, thank you," and "Help me, help me, help me." That's not as simple as it sounds. When we say, "Thank you" to God, we start realizing there are more things and people to be thankful for than we supposed, even things that are really surprising when they occur to us. And when we say "Help me" to God, it can lead us to look more deeply into ourselves and what we really need help with, and then it goes on to other people who need help.

Q: What about answers to prayer?

A: That's a mystery. I believe I do get answers, but they aren't necessarily obvious. A brilliant friend of mine told me once that he was outside one night and prayed that a sign of God's existence would appear in a particular quadrant of the sky. Right then, a shooting star went across the designated portion of the sky, and my friend said to himself, "Wow, what a coincidence."

I suspect something like that happens with our prayers. Usually things happen as a result of so many factors, it's hard

1. *1 Samuel 3*

to say that only one of them is *the* reason. But it would be foolish to say that God is not one of the factors—probably the major factor—in an answer to prayer. God just isn't obvious.

Perhaps the most critical "answer" is in the making of the prayer itself. When I take the risk and wager that Someone is there connecting with me, that in itself helps settle my spirit. It's like throwing out a lifeline and asking somebody to take hold of it and sensing that Someone does. Sometimes the "answer" is in just hearing what I said or thought differently and believing that Someone must have heard and given me that feedback.

It also helps me to pray more honestly when I know that other people, who have covenanted together, are also praying about what they're scared of, or wrestling with, or ticked off about, or whatever. It helps me to know others are trying to be aware of and respond to God as the eternal context for our lives. That kind of praying is personal but not entirely private, and the connection is an answer in itself.

Q: I have a question about being ticked off at God. What do you mean by that?

A: What I mean is that there's no point in hiding or covering over anger with nice words, if anger is truly what we're experiencing. God knows, literally, that sometimes, we get angry at God. Why we're angry doesn't matter as much as confronting God with it, not letting it fester or distance us from God, or poison us and our relationship with God. I think it works the same way with God as it does with each other in that regard.

To be honest about our anger with God, and to rely on God not to punish or cut us off, is to trust God and is a critical step toward building greater trust. Remember, it was hypocrisy that Jesus came down hardest on, pretending to be what we aren't. I also think it's a dead end to let our anger turn into a withdrawal or big sulk, or . . .

Q: Wait, wait. I have to ask you something—or tell you something. I've always prayed, a lot. But I'm so furious at God right now. I did pray, for a long time, about my own pain, and the family pain, and I did all I could think to do to try to redeem the hurt. But the hurt hangs on and is costly to me and the people I love. I don't know what to do with this. It's either let go of praying to God, or just talk to Jesus. So I talk to Jesus. What do you think about that? Maybe I lack faith.

A: Most change happens more slowly than we like in our "now is almost too late" culture. And there is a "quick, once and for all" idea about healing that can come from the biblical stories about Jesus and have become part of the Christian tradition. I believe God can do whatever God decides to do, but I don't think God works that way most of the time. The crunch comes when we can't see that God is doing something we want *now*, then we assume God isn't doing *anything*. Take heart. There may be more change happening in you, and your family, than you realize—or than you give yourself, or them, or God, credit for. Since more change occurs from crisis than intention, change may be happening in you and your family through your crisis.

We tend to think of faith as though it were some commodity, something we have or don't have. I think trust is a better word because trust implies an action. It is something we *do* rather than something we simply *have*. It is trust that nudges us to try something new rather than squeeze back into old ways and repeat something familiar that isn't working. Even a little trust helps make something different possible. It seems to me that you are trusting by continuing to pray in whatever way you can, and working for what you pray for in every way you know.

One of the faith affirmations we say together is that "Jesus is the chief clue to who God is and what it means to be human and faithful." I think by praying to Jesus, you are in the process of finding out how true that is.

Q: As you talk, I keep remembering that I grew up with a plaque on the wall that said, "Prayer changes things." I was taught to ask God for things and if you don't get what you ask for, then there's some other condition attached or some judgment in it. If you don't get what you ask, it's because you're bad or don't have enough faith. So it's hard for me to pray personally for specific things, and I end up sort of amorphously saying, "Be with me" or "Bless me." I guess my question is, "How personal is prayer?"

A: That dilemma that makes us all squirm a little. Maybe there ought to be a plaque on all our walls that says, "God answers prayer in four ways: 'Yes.' 'No.' 'Maybe.' And, 'Are you out of your mind?'"

Think about it for a minute. Prayer happens between personal beings, however asymmetrical the exchange. It's always relational in addressing the Other. Jesus consistently taught us to be direct, honest, and persistent in prayer: "Ask, seek, knock" and you will "receive, find, enter." So our chances of getting what we ask for are better if we're open and direct about it. Plus, in human terms, honest asking nurtures our relationships rather than expecting friends to read our minds. And asking friends makes it easier for them to ask us for something. It makes both parties freer and closer.

Q: Sort of *quid pro quo?* You think that's how it works with God?

A: Not exactly but a little, because I believe that God does want our trust, our love—love of God and neighbor and enemies, care of the earth, and concern for the poor and oppressed. But there is never a true *quid pro quo* between us and God.

Nor is there an exact, equal *quid pro quo* that applies between human beings. Friendship really isn't about keeping score. It's about nurturing honesty, openness, and mutual trust.

That's how it works in our relationship with God as well. I think prayer is the acknowledging that we're related to God in everything and all ways. If *nothing* can separate us from the love of God in Christ Jesus, then it's also true that *everything* links us to God. Prayer is a basic way of finding what that means in our lives.

Q: I'm not sure how we relate to each other also applies to God. Can you say more about that?

A: First, I'd say that no analogy from human life could apply absolutely to God because there is only one God, and that makes God incomparable. But there are things from our side that can point toward how God is and is in the world. Take language, for instance. The Bible says that God spoke the world into being. God spoke the commandments to Moses. God spoke through the prophets. John's Gospel proclaims that The Word was with God before it was made flesh. Language has the power to create or tear down, to open truths up or shut them down, to lead toward justice or toward injustice. We know that from our experience.

The point is that whenever anybody tells us a truth, that makes something different possible for us individually, and between us and them. Whether the truth is a personal one, or a relational, scientific, literary, historical, or social one, the power of language is that it makes something different possible for us humans. Prayer is language, even if in thought, silence, art, or music. If we don't we don't "speak" our truth, we shut off possibilities. If all we do is schmooze in charming ways, nothing different becomes possible.

When we honestly attempt to say or do something very hard, it changes things—not always or inevitably, but possibly. And most certainly it does that for the one who speaks and is no longer living by pretense or by infantalizing or idealizing those to whom he or she speaks.

So let me tell you a story about a father. It's about my father and me. I think it applies to my relationship with God, but I'm still working on why and how it does. Maybe you can help me with that.

My father was a very strong, tough man and never seemed afraid, never admitted to being afraid. But I was afraid. Often. Whenever I mentioned that to my dad, he would say, "Pull up your socks. Don't be a baby." Things like that. But my socks never stayed up. My fear handicapped me because I kept thinking something was wrong with me for being afraid. I'd never be the kind of man I thought my father was. My anxiety was like having a constant, low-grade fever. It didn't stop me from doing anything, but it made everything harder.

After college I came east to seminary and stayed on the east coast. My dad and mom lived in Oregon, and I made annual trips to see them. On one trip I was forty-eight-years old and in the midst of my divorce. My dad was seventy-five, and my mother was afflicted with Alzheimer's disease. Dad and I talked about Mother's situation, and we talked about my divorce. I told him then about being afraid as a kid, and how his response made me feel inadequate, how I always felt I had to prove myself, and how that screwed my life up in some ways.

My dad put his arms around me and said, "Ted, I've been afraid all my life. I should have told you. I needed to tell you. I'm sorry."

My first reaction was, "Why didn't you tell me that when I was a kid? It would have made a huge difference. It probably wouldn't have made me less afraid, but maybe I could have accepted my fear—and myself—better, sooner. Maybe I could have pinned my fear to the mat more rather than let it pin me to the mat so often."

My second reaction was enormous gratitude for my father's courage in telling me that day. He hadn't put his arms around me much before, but he did that day. What he said had broken down some barrier in him, and between us. In that moment I began seeing him for who he was, a brave man, not so much a tough, fearless guy—as if there really are any. I realized how much courage it took for him to get his family through the Depression, then World War II, then in mid-life risking a change of jobs and moving his family from South Dakota to Oregon and starting all over again, and now caring for my mother with Alzheimer's. I threw my arms around him, too.

I think this father-son story touches on our relationship with God and what prayer is and does. It's a kind of parable about humans and God and the power of words to make something different possible. If we trust, in whatever mustard seedy way we can, that God is there, loves us, works in life in mysterious but gracious ways, and we "ask, seek, knock" for as long as we live, things do change. In us, for us, for others.

Q: But doesn't it take more than just speaking, language, or prayer for things to change?

A: Sure. But action needs to be rooted in something. Words help us find and define that something. As Elie Wiesel says, words can be deeds. That's true, isn't it? Change can happen when we say hard things to a spouse or kid, neighbor or boss, public figure or whomever. If we challenge someone about a controversial issue, those kinds of words are deeds that can change things. So are words of compassion, mercy, hope, encouragement, instruction, inspiration. Often we become answers to our own prayers by extending them in our words and actions with others.

Which is to say that if we really want change, often we have to join in working for that change. We have to take up our bed and walk. Remember the parable about praying Jesus told his disciples in Luke 11? He told them about a guy whose friend arrives around midnight, but the guy's cupboard is bare. So he goes to the neighbor's house and bangs on the door asking for bread. But the neighbor has gone to bed and won't get up to give him any. So Jesus said, if the neighbor won't cough up bread out of neighborly consideration, he'll finally do it if the man persists in pounding on the door.

I love that story because it both links and blurs the line between praying and acting. Persistence is the key to both. It's a little like the interaction between earth and capsules on missions into space. Scientists keep making small, almost imperceptible course corrections that end up helping the crew of the space craft get to the right destination. So when we persist in making little corrections along the way, it may seem as if nothing is happening, but after a while we find we've changed, and the whole ball game is different.

Q: I'm struggling with the whole notion of God. I was taught that we pray to a benevolent God, a Father we bargain with. But now I don't know what really is out there. When a crisis comes up, I instinctively start to pray. But I find myself asking, "What is it I am praying to?" Can you say something about that?

A: I think the problem really lies in how much uncertainty we can live with—or admit we live with, since uncertainty is the stuff of life itself. A lot of us assume that we should know more about things not only than we do but than we actually can. Certainty, including religious certainty, seems to me to be bought either 1) by exaggerating what we claim to know and ignoring disconcerting questions, or 2) shrinking life into somewhat manageable parts and avoiding other parts, which results in the illusion of control. Neither works, and neither is accurate to life.

When we can get past our addictions to certainty and our need for indisputable proof, and accept that mystery, and ergo uncertainty, is at the heart of human existence, we can live with more freedom and trust. Of course, we know quite a lot and are learning more. But in the larger sense, we don't know very much about many things, including God. To trust God is to put the matter of certainty where it belongs; with God, whose ways are not our ways and whose thoughts are not our thoughts.[2]

Even our human "ways" are complicated enough to preclude much certainty about them. Just look in the mirror and realize that you don't know everything about who is looking back. So it's not particularly startling that we don't know much about God. We could read the Genesis story of the fall as Adam and Eve's presumptuous desire for certainty, which we replicate in our lives. It's hard for us to be

2. *Isaiah 55:8*

okay, even grateful, for uncertainty and mystery. Our heads want certainty while our hearts wrestle with the reality of uncertainty. Our growing in spirit involves moving toward the freedom and empowerment of trusting truth *beyond* certainty—and grace within mystery.

Q: Is there really such a truth? Something beyond certainty?

A: Truth is not always something literal. It's larger than that. Who was it who said when a truth is too big to speak, you have to sing it? In a profound way, that's what music is about—and literature, poetry, and drama. They present the meaning of life as what is true beyond scientific proof. Is a photograph a truer representation of a person than an artist's portrait, or is it just different? Finally, the key is what truth claims us, and what we decide is right by living it out.

I remember being in London's Trafalgar Square once, and there was a statue of Lord Nelson way up on a column. I couldn't see much about Lord Nelson from where I stood. Then I discovered a small model of Lord Nelson's statue in a place nearby so you could see what was high on the column. Somehow the small model and the description next to it helped me appreciate the monument and a bit more of the truth of what Lord Nelson did for the English people at of the battle of Trafalgar. In a way, we can say it's something like that with Jesus. He was down here, and so we can look at him and see something of who God is for us.

Recently my daughter, Karen, asked me where I got a quote I used in a sermon years ago. I couldn't find it, but she and I remembered it was something like this: "I'd rather die forever following Jesus and what he believed than live forever as one of those who turn away from him." That's what truth means for me. It carries me on day by day. Maybe it's a truth that will carry you, too.

Q: About following Jesus. What does that really mean? I read my Bible, but what else?

A: That question has a lot of layers, doesn't it? It's impossible to parse Jesus out of the context in which he lived, died, and was resurrected. The main record of that is *Scripture*. But his context is also the *community of faith* he gathered across time. Our *reason* is involved, too, thinking through what Jesus means and reveals to and for us in our time. And our *conscience*, hardwired into us whatever its cultural variations, is a factor. What it means to follow Jesus lies in the mix of these four components that Protestants say constitute church authority.

I hope that in the church we wrestle together about what being followers of Jesus means. Following Jesus has to have relational meaning, a connection to a community of other followers, not necessarily in agreement but in accountability. It has to be thoughtful. It has to be just. It has to be something to help others.

Q: It seems evident that, for Protestants, anyway, Scripture is the foremost source of authority. Why is it so important for us?

A: One of the important things about Scripture is that it's dynamic, not dead. It is about a process that is ongoing. And that's also true of faith. That's why I disagree with the fundamentalist who insists the Bible is the literal word of God, delivered once and for all. The problem with that view is that it tries to squeeze the world into the Bible rather than engaging the world with the Bible.

But other Protestants believe that the words of the Bible are human words that bear witness to God's Word. That Word has many dimensions, many levels, not just one. So at different times and ways, it speaks to us differently. There is a critical difference between the Word and words. Think of the Word as the dynamic of "the Truth," and words as carrying pieces of the Truth, but never exactly, or completely, or finally. Therefore, the

Word of God and the very Being of God are intimately united, but the biblical words are of a quite different order of magnitude from God's very Being.

We know the Bible contains many different kinds of writing and was written in different times and different languages by different people. It's history, poetry, moral teaching, drama, letters, stories of and about people who understood life as a covenant with God. It has many dimensions, many levels, not just one. So at different times and ways, it speaks to us differently. The primary theme of the Bible is covenant, which is what the word "testament" means. The covenant between God and humans always includes everyone, everywhere, no matter our different languages or words we use.

Scripture comes from people who, at the end of the day, asked, "What happened today? What did we experience? What does it mean? What's God up to?" What they wrote expressed and pointed to an *ongoing process* between God and them in their history and struggles. So it resonates with us. It speaks to the process, the dynamic between us and God in our history, both personal and in our world. It is a compass, not a road map.

Q: But the Bible seems to refer to another world, one that was very different from the one we know and live in. Does it really have anything to say to us now?

A: I know it's tough to get into the Bible, to read it, to plow through genealogies and what seems like archaic laws about what to eat and where to put the unclean stuff, all of that. It seems like an alien world in many ways. But try to get what's behind all that.

The first words of the Bible are, "In the beginning, God created the heavens and the earth . . ." Then John's Gospel says it this way: "In the beginning was the Word, and the Word was with God, and the Word was God . . . and everything as made through him . . . " Well, who was actually there at the "beginning"? But the guys who wrote those words looked around and decided that there was meaning to all this, and it was bigger than they were. We get the same intimations the ancients got when they looked at the earth and the starry skies. Sometimes something shivers us—a sunset, a single wild flower, a child playing in the park or in the street, a thousand scenes, a thousand times. That shiver is awe, wonder, a primal feeling, a sense of overwhelming meaning and mystery at the same time. The writers of Scripture grasped that God is behind it all, that creation does proclaim the glory of God, that the laws of physics at play in the universe come from some intelligence. Scripture is about the truth of meaning, not just the truth of facts.

Q: When I used to study the Bible, especially the New Testament, I knew it was important for only one reason: To tell us about the events of this person, Jesus. But the Bible didn't get written until a lot of years and events later. Then a group of men who knew Jesus, or knew some who did, wrote it all down—probably with the help of some women! And then there were all those church councils where it was decided what was in and what was out as far as the Bible was concerned. What do we do with all that?

A: Well, from the beginning there were many sources that had a part in shaping the Bible. There were historians, record keepers, king's scribes, poets, prophets, to name a few from the Old Testament. The story of Jesus was passed on by the oral tradition and collective memory of the early Christian community. The gospel was also shaped by interpreters such as John and Paul who wrote versions of the meaning of Jesus' life. The Bible was a process that engaged people and evoked interpretation by theologians and scholars through the centuries and on into our time and the future. That adds to our understanding of Scripture.

I think what Hebrew Scriptures, or Old Testament, tell us is not so much a complete factual record, or detailed history, as it is a reflection of the impact God made on the people, history, and nation of Israel and its neighbors.

The same is true of the Christian Scriptures, or New Testament. Scholars have tried but we can never get back to "the historical Jesus" in any exact way. What we have is the impact of Jesus on those who knew him, believed in and experienced him, heard what he said and how he lived and died, and how they encountered him when he was raised from the dead. That is pretty compelling and catches us up in the story and calls us to respond.

I believe there are many layers of meaning and interpretations in and about the Bible, not just one. It speaks to me in different ways all the time. I don't feel trapped in an alien world when I read it. I feel jarred and juiced up in this one.

Q: I find it hard to read about Jesus and not know for if what I'm reading is actually true.

A: Well, probably the way to go at this is to substitute the word "meaning" for the word "true." The Bible isn't a scientific journal with replicable experiments to prove something. If that's what it takes to relate to Jesus, we are all stuck. But if the meaning of life and death as Jesus lived, taught, died, and rose resonates with you and your search for meaning, you're on a deeper level of existence than just the factual one. Then you might ask yourself what was in it for those who encountered and followed Jesus if it led to scorn, persecution, death. Why would they make up a story with that kind of consequence? Just the fact that people didn't write a cleaned-up, smooth-edged version of themselves, or a heroic, idealized version of Jesus, makes their accounts more believable and their experiences more relevant to ours. To search for meaning is to shift emphasis from objective to subjective, from literal truth to existential truth.

Q: But, Ted, Jesus didn't know that the outcome of what he did would be the Inquisition, the Crusades, a lot of other bad things. What do you think he would have done if he'd known that?

A: I think he would have done what he did. What he did was who he was. I believe he would have trusted, as he did, that God would bring something good and redemptive out of it. Besides, the bad stuff? That's *us*, not him.

Q: But bad stuff is still an outcome.

A: Yes, because God doesn't control everything. We're free to make choices and, so, to make terrible mistakes. But the key is in the resurrection—or resurrections. History suggests there's a resurrection to the Inquisition, if only because the final word isn't the Inquisition. The final word isn't Hiroshima; the final word isn't the Holocaust; the final word isn't Pearl Harbor or September 11th or the Iraq war. Yes, all those are real, painful, terrible, and evil. But none of the "bad stuff"—or, for that matter, none of the "good stuff"—is the end of God's world and work in it. It's the witness of the gospel that nothing can separate us from the love of God in Christ Jesus our Lord.[3] That's as much of a creed as I need. How about you?

Q: Sometimes I think that the secular world is more religious than the religious world. Do you think the church has been co-opted by poets, writers, artists, authors, dramatists who see the awe and the conflict between good and evil, and present it in a more accurate way than we do? What use are religious institutions now?

A: First, let's be clear: God isn't limited in any way to, or by, what you call the "religious" world. I would despair if I thought that were true. Our world can't really be divided into religious and secular segments. That distinction is not helpful. God is involved in and over everything.

That means God speaks through religion, but God also speaks through poets, artists, authors, musicians, scientists, other people

3. *Romans 8:38-39*

and cultures and countries. Ultimately, everything is sacred, even if sometimes it's unrecognizably perverted. There is something religious even about the guys who flew the airplanes into the World Trade Center, something that got twisted and tragically distorted by denying the sacredness of all life.

By the same token, we ought to look at ourselves and at the terrible retribution that we have inflicted on the people of Iraq. What about the children and mothers and fathers and grandparents killed there? Don't you think God calls us to some contrition about it and not so much proud flag waving and nationalistic posturing? It's religion that raises those questions in the political and national security arena. It's religion that, in the midst of war, confirms the sacred value of both the lives we lost on 9/11 and the lives lost by the Iraqi families and people. If we think power, nation, death, and disaster are the only course to take, then I suppose paying the enemy back, and then some, is the way to go. But that isn't a faith stance. Morality is more complex than that. The religious and secular are one world, but, as my friend Bill Coffin says, "The challenge is to let people know God 'n' country is not one word."

Q: But when you lose someone you love, a parent, a child, a friend, the grief is overwhelming. Doesn't it come out as anger as well as tears? Are you suggesting that what the country is doing in Iraq or wherever means our faith is weak or wrong?

A: Oh no! Grief is deep and human, even shared by many animals. I'm not trying in any way to demean, or to be reductionist, about the tragedies of life. However, I do think that grief expressed as fear and anger can easily be obsessive, blind, and misguided. I also believe that tragedies don't have the last word about us or the world. Through trust and the support of counselors, friends, and the community of faith, angry grief can become wise sorrow. It can lead to more inclusive compassion when we realize we aren't the only ones who know grief and loss. In our sensitized humanity, we can reach out to human beings we might have disregarded before. I've seen that happen.

I also know that great tragedies sometimes have been converted into, or even by, acts of amazing creativity and imagination in art, poetry, music, sacrifice, and generosity of spirit. Out of Pearl Harbor came the redemptive rebuilding of Japan. Out of World War II came the Marshall Plan for Europe and the United Nations. Out of the Holocaust came Israel, however clouded the outcome still remains. What can come from tragedies depends on our reworking grief and anger by faith, compassion, and creativity. It's about not losing our souls to gain the world. It's about being redemptive rather than vengeful.

Q: My struggle with that is where is God operating when I read the paper? When I see war and environmental abuse and gay-bashing as public policy, I want to dismiss our leaders by saying they're all jerks because they don't see things the way I do. But that makes me no better than they are. But if I say, "Okay, God is working through all this," I feel as if I'm tolerating or condoning what's happening. Where is my individual responsibility in that?

A: That is a dilemma. But while you're looking for meaning in this struggle, it will help to be aware that the *need* to look for the meaning in what's happening is one way God nudges us to probe beneath the surface and simplistic answers. At some point, it's human to ask, "Why doesn't God do something about this?" But, if you think faithfully about it, you might wonder if that question isn't what God is asking: "Why don't *you* do something about this?"

Remembering scenes of World Trade Center disaster, most of us asked, "Oh God, why?" That's a good question. One good follow-up question is, "Did we do anything to drive people to do this to us, however insane it was?" The 9/11 Commission's asked that question, among others, and in its early report recommends that we reach out to moderate Arab nations, aid them and not ignore or disrespect them or treat them as ignorant and primitive. Looking for the meaning of anything is not about sitting back and doing nothing but swearing and moaning. It involves persistent prayer, being active, taking stands, joining groups such as the National Council of Churches "Faithful America" or Sojourners.

Q: What is it that drives people in a society not only to do the suicide bomber stuff, but to condone it and encourage it?

A: There are probably dozens of reasons: a misinterpretation of religion. Their country and culture being ignored, exploited, disrespected. Criticism of what they see as our immoral lifestyle. Poverty and a gloomy future. Feeling exploited. Despair.

Most of us in this country are fairly comfortable, and we get upset by relatively small things like colds, computer breakdowns, or a cantankerous neighbor. But there are millions of people in the world whose kids are always hungry and sick, who don't have running water, or who live on pennies a day. There are millions who get written-off as being of little worth. The other day in a deli I heard a guy saying the Islam religion is a religion of hate, and its followers are a bunch of barbarians. One guy saying that in a deli is bad enough, but when millions of Americans and others believe that, it's pernicious. That doesn't make anyone love us, does it?

People in the Dominican Republic make about a buck *a day* for hand stitching a dozen or more baseballs that sell for two or three times that much in this country. What do you suppose they think of us? Similar things go on in many in Third World countries. Some insist that those people wouldn't have jobs if we didn't employ them. But it's still exploitation, isn't it? The people still live in poverty. Surely it's understandable that people like that resent and dislike us. Our shrugs hurt them as much as bombs, and neither make sense or are moral or faith responses.

Q: What do you say to church people who don't want politics in the pulpit, or anything else controversial, and who talk about the separation of church and state to justify their position?

A: I say that God doesn't separate faith and life, morality and the market place, prophetic voice and the public arena. Neither should we. Of course, we don't want a church state or a state church. But separation of church and state doesn't mean the church should back off and not address public issues and policies that affect all of us. I think it's irresponsible and unethical to be silent and lower our voices to raise our budgets.

People pay attention to faith stances. The black church was the driving force of the Civil Rights Movement. Right now it seems the Religious Right is the dominant voice in American politics. I think in part that's due to the rest of the Christian community whose timidity and silence allows the Religious Right to define the religious and moral issues of the day. Abortion and gay rights are moral issues, for example, but Christians are not all of one mind on these matters. The moral or religious position isn't *just* Pro-Life and banning gay rights. Some of us hold that the moral position is Pro-Choice and the equal inclusion of gays in the rights and privileges of the rest of society.

I think we are morally and spiritually irresponsible if we *don't* say our side in the public arena. Not arrogantly but letting it be known our faith position by saying, "Here's what I believe and how I see these issues and their implications." How can people learn or think about these issues if we don't speak out and challenge them?

It involves more than abortion and gay rights. It's about saying, "My faith in God has to do with how we treat the poor, how we educate our young, pay our teachers, maintain our schools, how we take care of the earth, how we relate to other nations and people. Those are things God calls us to be responsible for." To speak out on that basis is a kind of evangelism.

Q: Let me jump in before we close shop here. I realize that, statistically, I'm one of the richest people in this nation. But it isn't in just other countries but in this country that we are continually abandoning huge numbers of people to poverty. How can I make a difference, except in little ways?

A: We're back to where we began. It's easy to despair. But the real question isn't how much difference we can make, but what stands we are going to take. What communities of faith, justice, and peace are we going to be part of? How are we going to live our lives, and why, where we are? We never know if our decisions are right. For example, it doesn't help me to ask if my wife is the most beautiful person in the world. Who knows? Who cares? I asked her to marry me because I love and trust her. That's enough for most basic decisions.

The point is that our lives are shaped by the specific decisions we make, our choices among the options given to us, whatever they are—including how to help people next door and in the ghettos of society. So faith and love pick options and live them out. Who we are and the difference we make is in the specificities of our lives. And in the mystery of our not being alone. And in our little works being strangely multiplied. We trust that God will use our choices, and that's liberating and sufficient.

We've come to the end of our time today. Among other things, we've talked about prayer, so let's close with one.

Gracious and long suffering God, the mystery of you and your ways is deep beyond our comprehension, but in many ways you have shown us that you are trustworthy and merciful and present with us to the end of all days. We thank you for being present with us today. We thank you for the chance to be together, to share within our faith, the deep questions of our faith. We are grateful for whatever crumbs of truth and insight have come to us in our being together, and we ask that you would be with us to sort out what has been said, to discern what is worth holding to, as it holds on to each one of us. And we ask, O God of us all in this human family, on this little but wondrous planet, that we may find your truths not just in our heads but in our hearts, and live them out not just when it is clear and easy but when it is hard and murky as Gethsemane so we may, by your grace, experience resurrections from time to time, and in the fullness of time. We pray in the name and spirit of the Lord Jesus. Amen.

Second Sharing

We ended last time with a prayer, but let's gather around a prayer to begin this session.

For our sake, O God, you both hide and disclose yourself, for without trustworthy clues to who you are, we would be totally lost. Yet full knowledge of you would deny our humanity. So here we are, eager to explore as thoughtfully as we can, yet in the humble awareness of our limited capacities and your incomprehensible providence, how and where you disclose yourself. We ask you to so move among us that, by your grace, we may learn more of you so as to love you more deeply and serve you more daringly. Take now our minds and think with them, our hearts and open them, our wills and direct them. We ask this for our sake and the sake of this world you love so much as to be with it always and everywhere to heal and redeem it; through our Lord Jesus Christ in whose spirit we pray. Amen.

Okay, here we go.

Q: I'm not sure this is a burning question but . . . can I ask it anyway?

A: Smoldering questions are allowed—and smoldering answers, too. Right?

Q: Right. Okay, it's about Mel Gibson's movie *The Passion of the Christ.* It's a hot topic right now. One person asked my opinion, and I said I was mystified by all the brouhaha. What do you think of the movie and all the reaction?

A: Most of the reaction comes from people who think it's the most powerful religious movie ever made—and from those with the opposing view, including Jewish leaders, who raise the issue of the movie's anti-Semitism and how the movie portrays the Jews as the instigators of Jesus' crucifixion. The fact is, there is a lot of anti-Semitism in the Gospels, especially in John. The charge of anti-Semitism leveled against the movie, as well as the New Testament, has some awful validity. Christians need to ask for forgiveness for that and its dreadful historical consequences for the Jews over the centuries.

The likely interpretation of what happened is that Jesus stepped on the toes of powerful people and entrenched institutions of both Israel and Rome. That view is also part of the Gospel accounts. Jesus bearded the lions in their dens, and they snarled back at him. While the people flocked to him, leaders plotted to stop him and started a whisper campaign against him. That happens even today when established power is challenged. Truth gets twisted—"spun" is the contemporary word—and that has cruel consequences.

Q: What often bothers me is why the crucifixion is such a big part of the New Testament and the church, and why the cross is the primary symbol of Christianity. Why the stress on death and not on life?

A: That's certainly a core question. Thousands of books have been written about it. The first thing to say is that Christianity is absolutely about life. Jesus referred to it as life *abundant,* life "deep and wide," as the old gospel song has it, with faith, hope, love, courage, humility, joy. Christianity is about those goose-bump moments when we experience life as a gift from God, whole and holy and "totally awesome," as kids say.

What is crucial, though, is that getting to that kind of life, experiencing it even a little, involves dealing with death. The mystery is that such life is yoked with Jesus' death because Jesus' crucifixion is inseparable from his resurrection. Abundant life isn't about going around death; it's about going through it, beginning with the fear of it and the suffering surrounding it. What buckles the knees of our religious fidelity and moral resolve is death and the threat of it, not only the literal big one at the end but the figurative little ones along the way.

By God's grace, Jesus revealed that life really is stronger than death. Faith is the process of wrestling and limping toward that conviction and becoming less afraid to take risks for the kingdom along the way.

A lot of us who consider ourselves "enlightened" Christians have trouble with the parts of the Gospels that are not about Jesus' teaching and moral example, since those are our preferred ways of relating to him rather than as a miraculous healer or one who sacrificed himself for us and was raised from the dead. So we move directly from Palm Sunday as a quasi-political event to celebrating Easter as the ongoing "renewal" of life in nature's spring cycle and a symbolic triumph of the values exemplified in Jesus. We tend to find stories of the agonies and death of Jesus unhappily tragic but not particularly relevant, and those of his personal resurrection happily inspiring but probably exaggerated. But that leaves the deep realities of life and death unaddressed, dismisses the cross, trivializes faith, and marginalizes God. Do you see that?

Q: About us? More or less, but I don't think it fits exactly. I mean, now we know more about the part mind and spirit play in healing, so Jesus' healing miracles, at least, resonate with most of us. It's someone dying for our sins that seems kind of far fetched or something. How could something that happened so long ago really relate to us now?

A: Let's back up and look at the crucifixion as it relates to the rest of Jesus' life and teachings because we can't unhook them. It's critical to keep in mind that when Jesus was teaching and healing in relative safety in Galilee, he *chose* to go to Jerusalem to confront his adversaries, knowing that it would likely lead to his death.

Jesus' decision and its consequences mean the last days of his life were the ultimate disclosure of who he was and what he was up to, as well as revealing more of God and how God works in the world. Jesus showed that confronting his enemies was what loving them was about. The events around the crucifixion are critical in defining Jesus as more than a teacher or healer.

Perhaps a majority of Christians don't think much about what the crucifixion means except as the way Jesus was put to death. So when we receive the bread and cup of communion, and the minister says, "This is my body . . . my blood . . . given for you. Eat . . . drink this, in remembrance that Christ died and was raised for you," the *"for you"* of the sacrament can make us uncomfortable. So we're inclined to reduce it to a memorial or maybe a kind of allegory. Sometimes it's even hard for me to celebrate communion.

Q: Communion makes you uncomfortable? I thought you clergy, of all people, got it, believed it, knew all about it.

A: Well, meet a mustard-seed man: "I believe, help my unbelief." Sometimes I'm uncomfortable because I live in the same time and world you do, with the same information challenges. And yet, I do mostly believe the reality of the mystery of communion and what it means. That's why I'm talking about it with you.

If we're embarrassed to think and share questions about the crucifixion and communion, and why they are central to the church and Christians, we lose by trivializing our faith and ourselves. And not only us, but those who think there is only one way to view or be grasped by the cross. There are many powerful ways to think of and experience the crucifixion, and we need to explore those ways together.

Q: Are you suggesting that unless our faith is rooted in the crucifixion, it's irrelevant or hollow?

A: Basically, I am saying that. We need to be open to God's grace in Jesus' crucifixion and resurrection because they're so intimately connected to each other and everything he was and is, and because they're so powerfully relevant to the depths of our lives. Begin there, then go on.

Let's risk jumping into deep water here. Christians believe that God was with Jesus in his life *and* in his crucifixion. What does Jesus' suffering say about God? What does it say about our suffering?

When we suffer physically or psychologically, we might say, "Why me? Why did God let this happen? Has God abandoned me?" So did Jesus. Some people say, "There must not be a God or these things wouldn't happen." Most of us ask, "Why are children born with a deformity? Or get cancer? Or get killed in car accidents or drive-by shootings?" The list goes on. Now it's, "Why did God let 9/11 happen?"

Our belief in a good, loving God gets challenged when suffering crashes or shootings oozes into the picture. Not many of us do very well with suffering—our own or anyone else's. But if, as Christians believe, God in some mysterious way really was in or with Jesus as he got nailed to the cross, then we can also believe that God is not absent from us when suffering comes and that God is able bring a kind of resurrection out of it. This makes it possible for us to discern and experience suffering differently; not eliminate it or dispel the mystery of it, but accept it differently. *God is in it with us,* even if we don't know how. That's essential to the good news of Christianity, and that truth isn't changed by the fact that Jesus' crucifixion happened two thousand years ago.

Q: As a young girl, the message I got about the crucifixion, and have been stuck in ever since, was somehow that it was my fault, even before I was born, this man got killed. The emphasis was that Christ died *because* of our sins as much as *for* them. We were told to dig our fingernails into our palms until we couldn't stand it, and know that it was worse for Jesus. As an adult, I've visited churches where hell fire is threatened for all who don't repent and repent and repent. My question is, what's that approach to sin about?

A: Responding to that question is a little like tugging on a single loose thread and having your entire sweater fall off. But I'll risk it.

Primarily, the issue is about "sin." I don't agree with the version of it you refer to, but it still makes an important point. The concept of original sin underscores something we too easily overlook, namely that sin is not just a personal or individual matter. It is also social, relational, and collective.

Take the sin of genocide of the Indian people in this country, or the sin of slave trafficking and using African people as slaves, or the pollution of the earth's environment, to name just three examples. The terrible damage, exploitation, and suffering inflicted on Native Americans, and African slaves and their descendants, corrupts our shared history. We have also ravaged the earth, air, land, and water in ways that seriously endanger our common home and future generations.

Though we didn't personally or directly commit those sins ourselves, we are complicit in them. We share the advantages and destructiveness those sins passed along to us, and in some sense we collude in their perpetuation. It isn't easy for us to grasp that because we so strongly emphasize individual responsibility and reward. And yet every parent experiences some sense of complicity when their kids do things that hurt others. I think if we put our minds to it, we could make a list of sins that we've been complicit in.

Q: Okay, but how can we undo those kinds of sins? They're in the past.

A: First, we should realize and confess our complicity in them and how they warp us spiritually and morally. I don't mean confess in a contrived *mea culpa* way, saying "I'm sorry" while counting the haul we got from mugging someone. And not in some masochistic variation of constantly digging our fingernails into our palms. I mean confession in a way that seeks forgiveness for the sin and faces its consequences.

Part of what original sin means is that since we are inexorably joined in sin, we also need to be faithfully joined in repentance. Repentance is not only to talk the talk but to walk the walk by turning around, changing course, and changing the consequences of sin. So we need to work toward the justice that repairs those consequences. We can't undo the sins, but we can undo at least a little of the damage those sins have done, and still do, to people. We can do something about entrenched systems of racism. We can stop exploiting Native Americans. We can stop being indifferent to the oppressive conditions that keep poor people trapped in poverty, and we can help change those conditions. We can press for reducing use of fossil fuel and promote using renewable energy to reverse global warming and its threat to humanity.

That kind of repentance applies to all kinds of sin against God, any time we do not love God with all our heart, mind, soul, and strength, and our neighbor as our self. Out of that sin, we exploit and oppress those I just mentioned. I could add other examples. There are a host of consequences of our corporate, as well as our personal, sin. Not to do anything about those consequences is to reinforce them. It seems to me that's why the prophet Micah calls us to do justice and love kindness and walk humbly with our God.[1] Even among Christians that view might not get a majority vote, so we and the church need to keep working on it.

---

1. *Micah 6:8*

Q: Why not just deal with my own sins? What's the point of dwelling on original sin or the sin of others?

A: Of course we need to deal with our own sin. But it's inadequate to focus just on our own because that overly privatizes faith and morality. It ignores how we collude in the larger social sin and its fallout. Sin, like life itself, is relational. Jesus taught his disciples to pray using plural pronouns including this line: "And forgive us *our* debts as *we* also have forgiven *our* debtors."[2] I don't think Jesus is referring just to reciprocity in forgiveness but to complicity in sin. Even as with faith, so with sin: It isn't just yours or mine, it's *ours*. And it's ours not just in the present but in the past and future, since the consequences of both faith and sin reverberate in time. Unless we try to change those consequences, all we do is pass them on. That's part of what original sin means and why repentant actions are integral to the process of being forgiven and forgiving.

We debate about *sins:* what exactly they are and are not, which apply to all cultures and which to only some, which are just "bad" and which are really "terrible." But the critical issue is not sins; it is *sin. Sin* generates sins. Sin is the chronic disorienting tendency in us all that causes us to overreach, seeking to be like God, or to underreach, settling to be like animals. Both are ways to deny the limits and gifts of being human. Sin gives us a bad case of the jitters about who we are, and our place and purpose in creation in the face of the great uncertainties of it all. It keeps us flailing around, groping for some balm for our jitters.

Sin is the distortion of our sense of our true proportions—and God's. Think about the story of Adam and Eve in the Garden. I think it points to what sin really is: *Adam and Eve wanted to be like God.* That's distortion of proportion in a nutshell. In fact, a double distortion. Without that distortion of proportion, they wouldn't have been snake whisperers and fallen for the snake's seduction.

2. *Matthew 6:12*

Our *sins* are the result of our reach for self-inflations, such as status, power, domination, money; or racial, religious, gender, or national superiority. Or of our stoop to self-regressions, such as addiction to things like alcohol, sex, consumption, lying, violence, cheating, pandering. But sooner or later that groping dehumanizes us and compounds our jitters.

Q: It's easier to think of sin as just breaking the rules: "Thou shall not kill, or commit adultery, or steal," or, I don't know, "covet"—though I have trouble with the last one, if lusting is included in that commandment . . . just kidding!

A: No, you're not. At least I hope you're not. You've just helped locate where sin lives in us. It's in the urge as much as in the act. Urge hatches act. So no urge, no act. I think that's what Jesus meant when he said that to lust after a woman is to already commit adultery with her in your heart. That's why the line in a great, old prayer of the church is so right on: ". . . cleanse the thoughts of our hearts by the inspiration of your Holy Spirit . . ." In a profound way, it is less the head than the heart that has the thoughts that really shape us.

Q: Yes, but really, committing the act is worse than having the thought, isn't it? Otherwise we'd all be in jail or something.

A: Physically, yes, acts are worse than urges. Spiritually, I don't know. I think what Jesus was getting at is that acts are fueled by urges and thoughts we all share. That levels the spiritual field. That undercuts false pride and self-righteousness. It exposes the *sin* beneath the sins, like the tough root of a dandelion under the yellow flowers that soon launch a hundred seeds.

Sin is the impulse, the nudge, or pull behind sins. Sin is the undercurrent below the surface sins, so to speak. Sin is the drive in us to act almost always, in everything, for what we impulsively consider to be our own self-interest, however

we may deny or disguise that impulse. Sin is the sly apti-
tude for holding that we are the center of everything. In our
"right mind" we know that isn't so, but sin subtly seduces us
into a "wrong mind." Even though we cleverly hide it, we get
rerouted into feeling, "It really is about ME, in spite of those
who criticize ME because they think it's really about *their* ME.
No, it's about ME and MINE—*my* ME, my needs, my view, my
money, my family, my race, my sexual orientation, my nation-
ality, my religion, my views."

Haven't you ever caught yourself thinking that where you
are is the center of the universe? I have, often. Then I drive
somewhere or fly somewhere, and I realize that, for those people, where they are is the center of the universe for them. What
I'm getting at is that we get so deeply hooked into our own
ME-centrism, it seems there's no getting out of it. Even a little.
And on our own, or by way of teaching and self-improvement
alone, there probably isn't. My belief is that out of a powerful and pervasive ME-ism, we keep doing things that are called
sins—acts that are damaging to others and a betrayal of our
true proportions as human beings.

**Q: That sounds rather hopeless and pessimistic, as if sin were
inevitable. So what do we do?**

A: Good question. I believe what we do is to stop pretending.
We begin by admitting our chronic self-centeredness. That's
the heart of confession, forgiveness, and repentance.

Let me tell you a story about that. While most of us rightly
protest violence, we know that there is violence in us as well as
around us. We don't like that, but it is true. We might not slap
anyone around, or whack or rape or mug them, but we often
hurtfully gossip about people, harshly judge them, cruelly criticize them, painfully ignore them, belittle them, exclude them—
even our children sometimes. Aren't those forms of violence to
people, perhaps not to their bodies, but surely to their psyches?

Add to that the news stories about a mother abandoning
her children to go get drugs, or a mother prostituting herself

for drugs, or a mother killing her baby. The news coverage of these tragic events usually implies or outright states, "How could any mother commit such a terrible crime?" In all honesty, any one of us could do such a thing. We don't, but it's not impossible.

So here's the story. When I was at Yale Divinity School, I remember one dark morning at three o'clock being *so* angry at my six-week-old baby son because he just *wouldn't* stop crying. I truly felt like killing him. I mean, the thought actually crossed my mind. I yelled "*Shut Up!*" and put him rather roughly down in his little crib. And then I cried. I was so upset. I felt I was some kind of monster.

Later that day, I went to a professor I liked and respected and talked about it. He said, "No parent who's honest will deny that thought has crossed their minds. It did mine with my babies. Give it a rest. And get yourself some rest."

That was a healing relief to me because people talk about how wonderful it is to have a child and how it's such a blessing. And that's true! But the flip side is that these little persons move into our turf, take over our lives, and don't even cooperate. Kids, babies on up, are both an absolute delight and a disturbing intrusion. We do get angry, feel hostile toward them, sometimes. It would help women if we talked about that, as well as about the joys of having kids. Otherwise, we almost demand that they be hypocrites, as we often are in our pretensions. The point is, denial and pretension hinder our admitting, recognizing, and intervening in our destructive feelings or impulses to keep from acting on them. I believe confronting our *sin* is a way to curb our sins.

Q: Isn't that more a focus on the value of therapy than of religion? What does it have to do with the crucifixion and Jesus dying for our sin?

A: To the first part of your question, I would say no. But it depends on whether you think of therapy and religion as radically separate categories. I don't. My personal experience is that God is at work in therapy just as God is at work in religion, medicine, law, and everything else. As a healing process, I consider therapy to be religious.

Q: From the point of view of my practice, I agree with that. What I meant to ask was not so much about therapy as about crucifixion and salvation. Isn't salvation about more than mental health? Why are you smiling? Did I say something funny?

A: I'm smiling because I'm thinking of a line from Edward Albee's play *The Zoo Story* in which one guy says, "Sometimes it's necessary to go a long distance out of the way in order to come back a short distance correctly." I remember that line because it often fits my experience—like right now.

Here we are in our discussion both a long distance out of the way and coming back a short distance correctly. You've asked a basic question, and there's no short distance way to answer it. And there isn't just one answer, except to say clearly that salvation is about more than mental health.

In talking about salvation, I believe we have to start with freedom. The whole creation is shot through with it. Freedom is a gift from God because freedom is what love gives. I think every person who has ever loved understands the connection between freedom and love. In having a created order that's independent of him/her, God risked suffering for us and for him/herself. Because we are free, we can really mess things up in our lives—and life itself.

We mess up for a lot of reasons. But I believe the main one is that we're afraid. Fear sort of hovers around the edges of our days and every once in awhile tromps to the center of them. We're afraid of something we can't fully name, but parts of it include being rejected, scoffed at, defeated, humiliated. We fear losing, especially losing ourselves, our lives, our loved ones. We're afraid of uncertainty, particularly the uncertainty and limitations of mortality and finitude. We fear all the contingencies that go with freedom. We're afraid of our freedom, of other people's freedom. We're afraid of the freedom of viruses to mutate, of cells to go wild, of synapses to misfire, whatever.

When someone said that love is the most frightening thing in the world, that's why. Out of love, God gave us freedom, and because we're free, we can distort our true proportions, miscast our place, and "fall"—several times a day. We can get into self-destructive feelings, thoughts, and actions. We can seriously hurt others as well through denial, betrayal, all kinds of mischief.

But out of that same freedom, we can also do all sorts of fabulous things: create symphonies, cures for cancer, wonderful literature, poetry, paintings, dramas, science, inventions that change our experience in, and of, life and the world. So when tragedies happen and people ask, "Why did God let this *bad* thing happen?" the answer is, "For the same reason God lets *good* things happen, good things we freely choose to create and do." We are free to love, too. And we do, at least a little. And just as the effects of sin touch everyone, so do the effects of our creativity and love.

Q: Okay, I can see how freedom gets us to the crucifixion, but where do we go from there? How does the crucifixion save us from our misuse of freedom, our ME-ism? Our sin?

A: As I experience and wrestle with the crucifixion—and with Jesus' life—it goes like this: Jesus' life and death were all about telling us—and showing us—that we don't have to be afraid. Certainly not of the all things we are afraid of, all those little deaths. Finally, he showed us that we don't have to be afraid of death itself. He struggled with all forms of death in his life, in Gethsemane, and on the cross, but he didn't flinch. Doing that, living that, linking it to his resurrection, "saves us" from having to hang on so tightly and fearfully to our skittish ME all the time. It empowers us to go on with trust from the crucifixion. Resurrection begins our exodus from slavery to fear and from ME-ism.

For me, trust is joined at the hip with courage. Or better, courage is the anchor of faith. I know it takes courage to trust, to step out on the promise. Without courage, betrayals come easily. I think that's at least part of what Gethsemane shows us: Jesus' courage. It trumped fear. It girded up love.

Q: But lots of people have courage without faith, don't they?

A: I suppose, but I think faith is around close enough for them to smell it. But I think trust is a better word to link with courage because it carries less ecclesiastical baggage. I'm not sure we can have courage without trusting something or someone enough to stand against our fear. And I think that's what the disciples came to, finally. You could say they trusted Jesus enough, past both their fears and their strengths, to believe in God. That's where salvation begins to go beyond mental health toward "being a fool" for Christ's sake.

What I'm trying to say is that the resurrection is inseparable from the crucifixion. Why? Because Jesus came back to the ones who denied him, who sniffled in guilt at cock crow and scrambled to save their own skins. But it was to them he came back. So at the core of the gospel, of the crucifixion, is not just the news that we don't have to be so afraid of death, but that even if we are, our fear can't separate us from God.

To trust that our fear doesn't separate us from God begins to break fear's hold on us. It makes us part of the resurrection now and that means we are free to loosen our white-knuckle grip on our ME. Jesus' crucifixion-resurrection sets us free to look at ourselves and the world differently, less fearfully, and to grasp that the world really is different than we saw before. That means we are free to take more risks, to care more about others, to be compassionate, hopeful, just, and joyful. That's enough salvation for starters, isn't it?

Look at the disciples before and after Jesus' death. Before, most of the time they were afraid of what Jesus was doing, what he was teaching, and where he was headed, even when they got bits and pieces of what it was about. After his death, meeting him again and seeing the nail holes in his hands, meeting him again on the road, in their cramped hiding place, by the sea in Galilee, they changed. They experienced him as the same One they knew before, but now they trusted him. Trusted what he promised. Trusted that he loved them. Trusted that those nail holes in his body meant what he said they did. Courage was a big part of that.

Peter and Mary and John and Thomas and Mary Magdalene and the rest were braver, more daring, more ready to go to jail, if that was what they had to do—even to die in trust—for love. I don't mean they were fearless, any more than we will ever be. But they were certainly much less afraid, and more forgetful of their ME. Because this crucified and risen Friend promised that he was with them to the end of the age and the ends of the earth, they took off into the world as different people. They understood that it really wasn't about them, it was about God. We're free like that, too, free to be much less afraid, to trust, to suck it up and step out. That's at least the beginning of salvation. And that's where we are *now*—on the road.

Q: I have to say that I've always labored under the . . . what? illusion? teaching? whatever I should call it . . . the notion that salvation is sort of a once and done deal. You're saved once and can date when it happened. You're sure of it. Like going to a revival and going forward to accept Christ. Anyway, I was never sure at all, never had that one, big-time experience. How do you know that isn't right about salvation? I hope it isn't, but how do you know?

A: I don't know it isn't right. I think for some people it is. But my experience is similar to yours on this score. But I'm pretty sure "once and done" isn't the only way, or even the primary way, to be saved. I don't think appealing to the fear of damnation is what Jesus did or is about. I don't believe the close-minded, high-handed way of such certainty is the way of trust or love or Jesus. When someone asks me if I've been born again, I tell them that on a good day, I get born again eight or ten times, on a bad day maybe five or six.

To me, being saved is a dynamic process. It's something we become part of and keep needing to happen. Remember the prayer: ". . . cleanse the thoughts of our hearts by the inspiration of your Holy Spirit that we may perfectly love you . . ."? We need to pray that daily, hourly. As Dizzy Dean once said when asked when he was going to pitch another no-hitter: "Boys, I'm good but I ain't perfect." Old Diz was right. None of us is perfect or ever acts from a single motive or a pure one. We're too complicated for that, too much a mess. So is the world.

So whatever it means to be saved, and all the consequences of that, it doesn't seem likely to me that it will be fully realized as long as we're in this world. We don't have to work *for* our salvation because that's a gift, and I believe God keeps giving it all the time. But we sure have to keep *working out* our salvation, according to Paul, with fear and trembling.[3]

By "fear," I don't think Paul meant the kind of fear we've just been talking about. I think he meant awe at God's holiness, awareness of God's grace, heart-pounding gratitude to God. I heard, or read, once that we've got to make our hearts big enough to hold all the wrong turns and hurts done to us and by us, or life shrivels up. I think being saved is something like having our hearts stretched more and more so they can hold not just the wrong turns, but the neighbors and enemies we're to love.

Q: I like that way of seeing it, but there's something about it that seems too easy or something. Like, anything goes with God. How would you answer that?

A: I'd say that's why the crucifixion is so critically important to us. Through it, God suffered, then he suffered for our sin, for the betrayals and hatreds and institutional corruptions, for the perversion of religion, the cruel behavior, the arrogance, for the whole mess. Suffering for something doesn't mean that the causes of the suffering are easy or that "anything goes." In fact, there's a certain judgment in that suffering because it makes pretty clear what sin does and what it is, its effect on God, others, and us.

3. Philippians 2:12

I'd also say that because God is present in this world, because there is no place or time where and when God is not present, then God is not sitting somewhere with a scorecard toting up our transgressions on one page and our good deeds on another. That image of God is a projection of our fear. I believe the process of salvation is to set us free from that kind of fear. Salvation isn't "getting away" with anything; it's being free to give our loaves and fishes out of gratitude.

But God's working in the world also means resurrections go on all the time. Out of terrible events somehow God works to bring something redemptive, different, better. To work out our salvation seems to me to involve joining in that work, trying to heal wounds, make peace, do justice, love one another. I keep going back to something physicist Richard Feynman said about imagination, that we have to stretch it, not to imagine what is *not* there, but to grasp things that really *are* there. I take that to mean beginning to see or to imagine the world as full of kingdom possibilities that we missed before, and living toward them.

Q: You still seem to be sketching God out as being pretty gentle, as a God some might characterize as a good-natured, well-intentioned teacher. And a while ago you yourself said teaching alone wouldn't save us from sin, the ME trap. Doesn't it take something tougher or harsher to do that, like the threat of damnation or hell or whatever? What do you say to that?

A: I'd say threats to get people to change just to save their skin is not even a very subtle appeal to the greed for salvation. It gets us even deeper into the ME trap. I believe that core change requires the crucifixion in all its ramifications. I'd say the crucifixion is a pretty tough judgment. It's like having someone who loves you—a spouse or kid or parent—show you how deeply you've hurt them, and urge and invite you to relate to them differently. From experience, I assure you that is extremely hard, extremely painful. Being dunked in lakes of fire might be worse, but not much.

I'd say that since the dis-ease and disorientation that results from the insistence on ME somehow replacing God is the heart of sin, then seeing and admitting that dis-ease and disorientation, which isn't ever easy or over, *is* part of the dynamic of salvation. God's saving grace involves continually getting reoriented to each other and God's kingdom and is certainly tied to the hard judgment of all the cross means.

God judges because morality matters, actions matter, justice matters—justice not as punishment or revenge, as we often think of it, but justice as correcting, healing, reorienting us as a surgeon does for patients by removing diseased or broken body parts to restore them to fuller life. All of which is to say that I believe salvation is essentially relational, not just individual.

God is not an enabler or supporter of wrong, or hurtful, actions. Nor is God a co-dependent. God doesn't join us in berating others for the speck in their eyes while conspiring with us in ignoring the log in our own. God doesn't collude in behavior that is destructive to us and everyone else—unless you hold that granting us freedom is colluding in its misuse. From the first page of the Bible to the last, God is confronting people, calling them to take responsibility for their mistaken views of themselves, for denying what's going on in their lives, for rationalizing how their attitudes and actions hurt them and others.

God is saying, "Okay, you're free, and you *can* do what you're doing, but there is a price. The price is the mess you're in and your soul's ache at midnight. If you live like you do, there's going to be 'trouble right here in River City.' Or right here in Jerusalem, New York, Philly, D.C., Omaha, San Fran, wherever.

The mess we're in together is itself the judgment. If one way or another, we expect or demand that the world change to our liking before we step out on the promise, as it seems we often do, we're at a dead-end in life and faith. Unless we take responsibility for our messes, nothing much changes in us or for the world. When we do take responsibility, things begin to change. Our reorientation can start.

Q: I'm teaching Jane Eyre right now, and one word we're looking at is "passionate." I did some research on the word, and the most common definition of it is the one we all know. It's having fire in our blood, whether it's romantic or whatever. But the root of the word comes from the Passion of Christ and is related to the word "passive." How could Jesus' Passion be passive? Is it because Jesus allowed himself to be open to the suffering so it would transform him? Is that what we're supposed to do, too?

A: You're raising a good point. I certainly think Jesus was open to suffering. But it's difficult, if not impossible, to think of Jesus or God as being passive, or passive aggressive—which I don't have much use for even when I behave that way from time to time. I think Jesus was open to suffering as a possible outcome of his actions, but I don't think he sought it for its own sake. I don't think he was a masochist or a martyr. Nor do I think suffering was for his own transformation. It had to do with transforming us and the world. I believe his humility was not about passivity but a willingness to risk humiliation and to suffer for who he was and what he was.

Often wherever Jesus went, trouble followed. He seemed to stir it up. He confronted people, drove the moneychangers from the temple, exposed the authorities as hypocrites, taught things that upset traditional mind sets. He was willing to suffer if that was the outcome of what he did. Suffering came to him, he didn't go looking for it—except to heal it in the sick and in the system. If God is in some way uniquely present to us in this Jesus, God is also willing to suffer for and with us. If, in Jesus, God took the initiative to break through to us, then the word *passive* certainly wouldn't fit God either.

Q: You use words such as "if" God was "with" or "in" or "present to us" in Jesus. Could you take a moment and tell us how you see God's relationship to Jesus?

A: Let me give you a quick view, and we can talk about it more in another session if you want to. For me, and I am not being original here, the connection between God and Jesus comes down to two or three options. There is mystery about each of them, and they are not necessarily mutually exclusive of each other. So bear with me now.

The first, most traditional way is simply to say that God was in Christ. When we call Jesus "LORD," we're saying Jesus is essentially God. "LORD" is how the Jews referred to God because God's name is too holy to speak. The rub comes when we say, as Christians, that Jesus was fully human yet fully God. Most ancient creeds try to define how that is, but the words used are pretty abstract.

Those creeds and statements were made when human thought was limited to a more primitive view of the world, before science pushed the borders out billions of light years. So people thought in quite literal, materialistic ways, debating about how many human parts to God parts there were in the Jesus mix. Over time, people tended to shift the equation to more parts of one than the other until basically Jesus was said to be God disguised as a human being without really being one.

A second view is that Jesus was just a good man, one who taught us about God and moral behavior. In this view Jesus' relationship with God was about the same as ours, or whatever "good men" we point to in history: Gandhi, Mother Teresa, Martin Luther King Jr., other "saints"—people who stood firm in their goodness, were exemplary, prophetic, kind, compassion, heroic, willing to die for the cause. But they were only human, not God in any sense of the word. Those who hold this view protest calling Jesus "God's only son" because they see others as God's sons and daughters as well. They believe these special good people don't completely die, as we do, but live on, as Jesus does, in the lives of those they leave behind. That makes resurrection a powerful myth. It impacts our psyche enough for us to try to be good the way they were.

The third view, and the one that I find compelling, is that through Jesus and the crucifixion, God acted in a decisive, but not final, way. In Jesus, God revealed who God is and how God works in a *unique, but not exclusive,* way—as my Yale

Professor and theologian H. Richard Niebuhr said, and I keep quoting.

This, to me, is a more helpful way of seeing how God was in Christ. I think science, what little of it I grasp, suggests how this might work. I keep reading and trying to understand it, and I may have it wrong, but science talks about invisible fields that hold the universe together so that somehow we see a blip in a far off galaxy almost when it happens, not in the time it would take light to travel from that galaxy to ours. Quantum physicists talk about particles decaying into two particles, each flying off in opposite directions, and yet no matter how far apart they get, they stay connected and behave identically, simultaneously. If one whirls around on earth, the one on the other side of the solar system does the same. These occurrences suggest that there might be more simultaneity between separate subjects or objects than we've thought. They also hint at credible ways of understanding how God was in or with Jesus, and how God might keep working in the world in the same way now as he did then, but not as visibly or obviously as in Jesus.

Q: That's an intriguing idea. Do theologians or other people look at the relationship of God to Jesus in that way, as the one who shows us what God is like?

A: Barbara Brown Taylor touches on it in her superb and helpful book *The Luminous Web,* but I don't want to suggest she's responsible for my views. Others I've tried to read are *The Whole Shebang* by Timothy Ferris; *God: The Evidence* by Patrick Glynn; *The Pleasure of Finding Things Out* by Richard P. Feynman; *A New Science of Life* by Rupert Sheldrake.

I believe the crucifixion and the resurrection show ways that God is involved in human life and history. God suffers with us, and over us, and God works to make the suffering into resurrections. We've all had miniature crucifixion and resurrection experiences in our lives. We've experienced times when we've been absolutely devastated and, yet, something happens to lift us up and keep us going. Why? Because God, who did that uniquely in Jesus, keeps on doing it among us. God is present in many ways. Maybe those little incarnations happen when somebody reaches out and helps us, because God works in and through other humans, though not exactly like in and through Jesus.

God is in the suffering, the crucifixions. God is in the awe, the joy, the resurrections. God is also in the next chance, the emerging possibility, empowering us to risk that possibility of the kingdom. That's part of the mystery of Jesus and how God is present and working among us all the time.

I don't know if any of this scratches where you itch, but I do know that it doesn't answer many of the questions you might have about sin and salvation and the cross. There are always a lot of questions left over when we go deep into our faith.

Q: Here's a question I have. Wasn't it God's plan for Jesus to be crucified?

A: I believe God knew it was a possibility, an odds-on possibility. But not a certainty. So, no, I don't think God planned the crucifixion; people planned it. But did God turn this horrible event into something good? Of course.

Q: Then what does it mean that God gave his son so we wouldn't perish? Isn't that a plan?

A: In a general way, yes. But God's gift of Jesus to us, and Jesus' gift to us, was freely given, to be freely accepted. We didn't have to accept the gift of Jesus, and we didn't. That was our choice, not God's.

The core issue you raise is what kind of a God do we glimpse in Jesus Christ. Is it a God who controls everything? That would cancel out freedom for us, for Jesus—even for God. There could only be one way for everyone. I don't see that kind of God in Jesus, do you? I see not a God who *controls* everything, but a God who can *cope* with anything. I believe that nothing can happen that God can't deal with, but God doesn't determine what happens before it happens. I believe a coping God is more congruent with one who loves.

Q: Could you or would you say more about this notion of God's plan? I keep hearing people say they are looking for "God's plan for their lives."

A: I'll try. With a true story. When Bill Coffin's son, Alex, accidentally drove off the pier in Boston in a night fog and drowned, he was twenty-four. In a sermon about Alex's death, Bill said some well-meaning person had told him that Alex's death was God's will. Coffin told me later he could hardly refrain from throwing the woman out of the house where people had gathered after the funeral. In his sermon, Bill put it like this: ". . . God doesn't go around this world with his finger on triggers, his fist around knives, his hands on steering wheels. . . . My own consolation lies in knowing it was not the will of God that Alex die, that when the waves closed over the car, God's heart was the first to break."

That makes sense to me. If freedom is real, then we can do things of our own volition, and God doesn't know what we'll do until we do it. I don't think God *plans* what happens for us specifically for the same reason parents don't or can't plan everything for their kids. And yet, I believe God's *purpose* for us is steadfast. I think it's the same kind of purpose parents have for their kids. We purpose for them to learn, to grow, to become people who are happy, who help other people, all those good things. We try in lots of ways to get those purposes to happen for them. But what if they get hit by a car on the way to school and are paralyzed or killed? Or they become addicted to alcohol or drugs, or get involved in some criminal stuff? Or get raped, even murdered? That isn't part of our purpose, is it? But love doesn't control other people.

We're all free to do what we do, and sometimes kids go off in destructive ways we didn't plan on. And yet we hang in with them because we purpose for them something different than the tangent they've gone off on. Our deeper purpose is to love our kids, whatever happens. We cope with them the very best way we can because we love our kids. We suffer with them and for them. We do everything we can to help them get it right, live as fully as they can.

That's as close as I can get to what I believe is God's the Father-Mother's purpose for us and how God copes. And part of the mystery of it is that God hangs in with us and, in response to our disasters, offers new options we can choose. God, like a parent, is with us not to protect us but to help us get back from the kind of dead ends we get ourselves into. Even as we give our kids repeated choices to live more fully, so does God give us options. Though God's purpose for us is an ultimate one, the options are a gift. They're God's response to what we do, the good and the mistakes, the warts and all. That seems purpose or plan enough for me.

Q: But didn't God have a plan for Jesus? Wasn't he born to die?

A: In my view, no differently than any of us are born to die.

Q: But Jesus died a special death, didn't he? Isn't that why we're talking about the Passion?

A: Certainly there is a special quality to Jesus' death, yes. Or, better said, the way he died. But that doesn't translate into saying that his death, or the kind of death he experienced, was prescribed from the beginning. Of course, that's one way to look at it. And there are some references in the Bible that say something like that. But, for me, the specialness is in the way Jesus lived as well as the way he died. He was crucified for being who he was. In him, God confronted us, challenged us, then entered into our suffering and death and changed it. Jesus linked it all to God's love, not God's control.

When I was a kid dragged off by my mom to our little Methodist church, people didn't say the line in the creed about Jesus descending into hell because "hell" was a swear word. So it wasn't until years later that I became aware of that omission—and that I'd missed something powerful about that censored line. I think that Jesus' descent into hell affirmed that even people in hell are not separated from God or beyond God's reach. To me, that speaks of God's freedom to do new things. To cope.

God coped with Jesus' death by bringing life out of it, even for those in hell, so to speak—which means us in our various versions of hell as well. That's what makes Jesus' death and descent into hell special. God coped by the resurrection. I hang on to that because it means no matter how hellish I think things are, I'm still not separated from God, and neither is anyone else.

Q: Just one more question from the marrow of my conservative upbringing. How could atonement happen without Jesus' sacrifice?

A: I don't know. But I keep saying that the crucifixion involves not just Jesus' death. His death and his life are inseparable. The atonement involves both.

Q: I hate to admit it, but I've never been clear about what atonement is. What does it mean? I suppose that's Christianity 101, which I must have flunked.

A: No, no, it's graduate school Christianity. Permanent graduate school. Most simply, atonement means repairing the breach or the estrangement between two parties. It can be between two or more people, or, in this case, between people and God. Atonement is bringing the parties back together, reconciling, restoring the intimacy. Usually there is some price to be paid for that, typically by the offending party . . . I'm sounding like a lawyer.

Q: So isn't Jesus' suffering and death the price that was paid for the atonement?

A: Yes, if we grasp that everything he did and taught was connected to his death . . . now I'm sounding like a broken record or a stuck CD.

To make atonement, it is commonplace for the *offending* party to pay the price, to make reparation. But the mystery of our atonement is that God, the *offended* party, took the initiative in Jesus to reconcile us. One way to see it is that God paid the price because we couldn't. Another way to view it is that God made Jesus the innocent substitution for the offending parties, us—the ones who broke the covenant by not loving God with all our hearts and minds—and inflicted on Jesus the punishment we deserve.

But for me, the most compelling way to understand it is that God took, and keeps taking on—or in—his/her broken heart, the suffering our sin causes us and others. God reworks it, invites us to join in the reworking and what cost that involves—and what love and joy as well. Paul says God made us ministers of reconciliation, and I think that's about as good a description as any of what Christians are about.

Q: I hear people say that God tests us in suffering, that suffering is necessary for faith to grow. Do you believe that?

A: I definitely *don't* believe God is in the testing business. Not like the gods of Greek mythology, or kids pulling the wings off of flies. Do I think suffering is *necessary* for faith to grow? Probably not. I don't think we have to go looking for suffering, but I think one kind or another finds most of us. That can either embitter us or make us compassionate. In that sense, suffering can, and often does, strengthen faith. To say suffering is *necessary* is to promote martyrdom, which is often an extreme version of egomania.

Q: You talked a little about the resurrection being part of Jesus' passion. The notion of resurrection really grabs me and confuses me at the same time. I understand some about spring and rebirth and new life. But when it comes to the resurrection of the body, I get stuck. What do you do with that?

A: Oh man, we've only got a little way to sail to the end of our session, and here's another depth charge to rock our little boat. I hope we don't capsize on this one.

In the first place, I don't think it means that the literal, physical body is resurrected. I had a secretary once who used to talk to me about the Rapture, you know, that all of a sudden some born-again folk would be taken up to heaven in a blink of an eye, and others left behind. She was sure she'd go up, but she was worried about me. One time she asked me if I thought the Rapture would include dead people, too. I remember saying I didn't know. But to kid her a little, I asked what if some worms ate part of the body, and then a bird ate some of the worms and took some back to the baby birds in the nest, and they got big and flew away, and a cat caught and ate one of them, and the cat's family moved across the country . . . you know, I went through a big routine. Then I asked her how that dead person's body would get pulled together to be raptured. She got quite upset with me.

And she missed the point, which is I don't think whatever the Rapture refers to, or more particularly the resurrection, it is about *physical* bodies being raised up, at least not the exact physical body that entered the grave.

Q: So what do you think "body" means vis-a-vis the resurrection? Wasn't Jesus' body raised from the dead?

A: Slow down a minute. When you think about what a body is, it can mean different things. It's flesh and bone and blood. But more specifically, it's a definition in space. A body is what distinguishes one of us from another. It makes us recognizable as who we are and where we are. Without bodies we couldn't relate to each other. We'd be neither here nor there; we'd just melt into one big blob of whatever. Even scientists talk about the universe as being a network of relationships. As far as humans are concerned, we need bodies of some kind to be part of that network.

Bodies are also about boundaries. They suggest that there are limits to our being. We're not now, or hereafter, just floating spirits with no boundaries. Only God can be everywhere. Bodies also represent some continuity in life between now and then. Jesus' wounds in his body, for example, enabled the disciples to recognize him as who he was.

So what's raised is a *person*. In Judaism, body-mind-spirit are one whole being. It's the Greeks who divided them up into more or less discrete parts, and we have done the same thing. Now there is a new understanding of just how interrelated body-mind-spirit are: We're persons of a unified body-mind-spirit. Medicine is finding that out in the recognition and treatment of disease.

So it isn't much of a leap to imagine the resurrection of the *body* as meaning the resurrection of a *person*, not just as flesh and blood but as something that reflects mind and spirit in a new definition in space—what Paul calls "heavenly bodies," presumably without cracking a smile.[4]

Resurrected bodies make it possible for us to relate to each other. And relational stuff is the core of what love and justice and peace are about. So the relationships that we have here go on. The learning goes on. The struggle goes on. The growth in love goes on. And Jesus goes on with us. That's how I see it.

4. *1 Corinthians 15:40*

Q: I'm fascinated by what you're saying here. I mean, my soul really resonates to it. I think of so many ways. My parents are dead now, but I think of my longing to be with them. And my longing to be with my ex-husband, my kids, friends more deeply now. So can you say more about relationships going on?

A: I never shared my truth with my mother and father, never shared who I was, stripped of all the idealization and pretension everyone in our family bought into. Mom and Dad both died before I could muster the courage to initiate that conversation. I really regret that we never got to the level of relational honesty and openness that would have been important and healing to us. It means so much to me to trust that such healing and intimacy could still come in God's kingdom past death.

To have a relationship go on is to say that the possibilities remain. As long as you and the others you mentioned are alive, the possibilities are there. I hope you can muster up your courage and not miss those possibilities. But if you do—and all of us probably miss at least part of them—the possibilities go on after death, I think. As they did for Jesus and the disciples. Maybe it takes forever to realize those possibilities, to find the peace, justice, love, and joy that we most deeply long for. But I trust that longing is not just about something in us but something about God. I think God is in our longing, that God has put it there. And will not leave it unmet.

Q: That's pretty powerful stuff. But where does that conviction come from?

A: Well, for instance, I believe every child, every parent, every brother, every sister, every friend, every enemy knows the separation, the alienation that is part of our common existence. And if we could, we'd do whatever it took to change that. So I just have to believe that since God is both better and more powerful than we are, God will give us the chance to go on in our relational struggles, give me a chance to go again to my parents at some point and do what I missed doing this side of the grave.

Do I *know* all this? No, I don't. But I think it's a possible, faithful way of understanding the resurrection of the body.

There's also Jesus' image of God's house having many mansions, or as newer translations say, many dwelling places. I've read that hundreds of times at funerals and wondered about it a lot. I've come to think it means that there are many rooms in God's house, or kingdom. To me it means that everything isn't all transformed in the moment we die and go to heaven, and somehow everything is worked out perfectly. Actually, I'm not sure that I, for one, would find that very attractive. I think I'd be bored, or after a million years or so, I would get that way.

So I think of the "on-going-ness" of relationships in two ways. One is this: All the creeds and the Gospels, whatever else they claim about Jesus, affirm that he was fully a human being, right? Then, it seems logical that the rest of us aren't quite fully human yet, doesn't it? I'm suggesting that in resurrection we continue to struggle to be fully human, not angels or whatever, but fully human, like Jesus. Sounds strange to say, but there it is. And to be a human being is to be related to other people. How else can that happen? How can we be related to God without that? To be *fully* human means that we're probably going to be working on it for quite a while.

The second way I think of "on-going-ness" of relationships has to do with an almost primal connection we all have to Jesus. The other day I heard a curious thing about Galatians, so I checked it out. And there it was. Paul tells us to have faith *in* Jesus.[5] But there's a little footnote that says the word "in" can also be translated as "of," and that suggests we can have the faith *of* Jesus. You see, there are different ways to hold to, and be held by, when moving toward and through death: faith *in* or *of*—and we could add *with*—Jesus.

Put them together, and you have a whole different realm or way of discernment about being fully human. To trust *with* Jesus is to hang on to the faith *of* Jesus, and thus to be held by faith *in* Jesus, whose teaching, living, dying, and resurrection were a promise to us that he would be relating to us to the end of always. That's where my hopeful conviction comes from.

5. *Galatians 2:16*

Q: What I'd like to know is what I owe God in more practical ways. I find that I prefer to talk with like-minded people. I have a really hard time with, and certain disdain for, people who are out there being faithful as they see it but espousing things that seem so contrary to what Jesus taught and did. I have a certain cynicism about those people. Am I called upon to talk to them? I mean, does my faith call me out in a way that's scary for me? That makes me feel foolish? When you talk about Christ, and Christ's crucifixion, I see myself as a person who would have been complicit in that.

A: We all would.

Q: Absolutely. And I would be complicit again, because I'm doing that same thing now: I don't speak out. So what am I called upon to do?

A: What you're asking is an ongoing struggle for all of us. It's easy for me to talk, and for us to think about these things together. But it is hard for us to live them, to trust in them, to let ourselves be changed by them. Let me list a few things I believe we're all called upon to do.

Start with this, literally: Pray! Every day. Don't believe those who criticize you for "just praying" instead of doing something. Don't believe those who complain that all they can do is pray and think that they should do more. Maybe they should, but prayer is a lot of the "all" anyone can do. A *lot*. Plus, prayer reminds us that we're not in this alone. So pray daily for what you believe: peace, justice for the world, hope, and courage. Pray for yourself, for your children, for all the children of the world. Pray for our president that God lead him in ways of compassion and humility and justice. Prayer does help deliver us from the temptations of helplessness or hopelessness. And it gives perspective that God's time-table is not ours. We frequently do not get what we pray for when we want it, which is probably a good thing. So keep praying.

Then talk to people. Talk about the issues of the day with all kinds of people, not just those who agree with you—except when you need a boost. Try to relate your faith to the subject. Tell people what you believe. Tell some of them that what they're saying about religion is not in keeping with the spirit of Jesus as you understand it. Period. Speak with humility, but be as clear as you can. I often ask the neo-cons I encounter, "What do you do with Matthew 25 about caring for the sick, the homeless, the hungry, the least of these, as you would for Jesus? What do you do about the poor because, very clearly, Jesus had a strong disposition for justice for the poor? How do you follow him in that? How do you do that if you're only talking about personal salvation? How do you reconcile your oppression of homosexual persons and racial minorities—or the bombing of Iraqi civilians, old people, mothers, and kids—how do you reconcile any of that with loving your neighbor as yourself and loving your enemies? Do those commandments trouble you in any way? How does what you say and do square with the gospel?" Don't give up the religious high ground to the reactionary religious people.

You never know what difference your words might make. I got a letter from the daughter of a former Archbishop of Canterbury. She told me that when her father died she went through his personal things and discovered he had my book *Guerrillas of Grace* on his desk, and it was absolutely threadbare. She kept it for herself. It's miraculous to me that one of my little books from my first small publisher touched the life of an Archbishop with who-knows-what influence. But you just never know. Just say what you think and believe. It's like the loaves and fishes that got multiplied somehow.

And at the same time join up with others who speak and work for the things you believe. Support them every way you can. All of us are in a position to write a letter or send an e-mail to our senator or representative. We cannot control the consequences of what we say and do, but we can look ourselves in the mirror a little longer every day. And, remember, God can't use loaves and fishes that we don't offer.

The last, or perhaps first, thing is to be active in a church and press it to get involved with the issues of the day, however controversial they are. Often a small minority controls the church because others let them. Churches need our voices and views of the gospel. We can learn from each other only if we challenge and hold each other accountable, and support each other in spite of differences. We all change slowly.

Q: I don't disagree with what you're saying at all. It just seems that nothing is enough. Sometimes I think maybe it's enough for me to be with my son and his wife, who spent years in fertility clinics and miscarried five times and just had a little baby daughter a couple of weeks ago. The mother had gestational diabetes and maybe the baby has it. It's a little thing to be with them, and yet it's a big thing. It's a big thing for me to have the time, thank God, to be able to be with them. Sometimes it's enough. I can't make it right for everybody. Who ever can?

A: You're on target. It is presumptuous for us to judge what is enough and what isn't. That's God's business. A few loaves and a couple of fishes were enough once, and who knows how many times since. When we, as Lincoln said, "Do the right as God gives us to see the right," that's all we can do. And it won't be right for everyone.

We are very little people in this world. We're not as important as all that, except to God and a few others. But we can be faithful where we are and with as many other people as we can. That *is* important. This group, this meeting right here is important, because we're here together. It's important to me because we care about each other enough to talk about these things together. What goes from here, in the lives of each of us, I don't know. But I know I'm different because I've been here. I just am. And that's the best I can put it. I know it makes a difference in ways we can never know. That's the hope for our loaves and fishes. Thanks for those that each of us offer all the time. And next time we gather, be sure to bring back your leftovers.

Third Sharing

O Holy One, though you inhabit eternity, you still infuse our time; though your thoughts are not our thoughts, you still stir our minds; and though your ways are not our ways, you still walk with us. We pray now for you to so sharpen our awareness that we may gather trusting your presence; to so excite our minds that we may dare to use them in your service; and to so open our ways to your bidding that we may find nourishment for our life with you and our neighbor. Assure us that awe of you does not preclude any questioning, that belief in you does not eliminate all unbelief, that hope in you does not ease every concern, and that you welcome us scruffy prodigals as your own. Assure us, as well, that your limitless love for us scrubs away need for pretense and frees us to ask from our hearts to yours, seek through our minds for yours, knock with our longing on the portals of your kingdom in the company of our brother, the Lord Jesus Christ. Amen.

I guess we're more or less ready now. So who has a question?

Q: I've been thinking about all the discussions these days about the impact of Christianity on our nation's history and politics. I just read an article in *The New York Times* by David Brooks that seemed to make a lot of sense. But afterward I thought, "Wait a minute, that isn't quite the case." Brooks said that there are times when religion determines the course of events, and he used the example of Martin Luther King Jr., who operated out of a Christian base. He said King insisted that the Civil Rights Movement wasn't a political movement with religious overtones but a Christian movement that had political ramifications. You were involved, so what do you think?

A: I think Brooks got it right about Dr. King. King's primary motivation was his faith, and that of the black southern churches. His nonviolent strategy was certainly religious, a mix of Christianity and Gandhi. Yet, I also think King and the leaders of the Southern Christian Leadership Conference were shrewd politicians, "wise as serpents and innocent as doves," as Jesus put it to his disciples when he sent them out "like sheep into the midst of wolves."[1] We can't draw distinct lines between a religious movement and its political impact. Certainly not all the people who participated in the movement were Christians, or even religious, but the black church was certainly the heart of it.

Q: I guess my question is not so much about King and the Civil Rights Movement as about the implication that Christianity has made such a positive impact on our country and history. Take Jackie Robinson. I lived in Brooklyn at the time, and I don't know whether Jackie Robinson was religious or not. But he certainly paved the way for a lot of black athletes and black people in other areas. And yet you can't really say that Christianity made that happen. I wouldn't say that every step toward justice or peace is because of Christianity, would you?

A: No, I wouldn't. At least not in the sense of all good things being traceable to institutional versions of Christianity. Christianity has taken too many forms for that to be true. It isn't monolithic. And yet, in some sense, I would be among those Christians who see all steps toward justice, peace, and inclusion as outcomes of the way God works in the world.

1. *Matthew 10:16*

Q: As a college student, I've noticed that Christianity, and religion in general, exerts a big influence in this society in general. I recently did a project where I examined homosexuality and how it is viewed in various denominations of Christianity. It was a very interesting study. The overall discomfort that society has with it really comes down to roots in religion, which for hundreds of years has viewed homosexuality as sinful, contrary to God's order in nature. As a Christian, I've come to realize that religion often has a strong negative or damaging impact on society. How do you see that?

A: I look at it in several different ways, not just one. In general, I think you are quite right that religion and institutional Christianity has often done great damage to the human family through things such as the Inquisition, witch hunts, crusades, slavery, pogroms, a sinful collusion in the holocaust and idolatrous nationalism. Some would frame the struggle with terrorism as a kind of religious war between Christianity and Islam, between good and evil. That is to badly miscast both religions. But most Christians and Muslims would not agree with that miscasting at all.

Nonetheless, there's a shameful, long list of damaging historical acts that have been done under the guise of Christianity or of a particular interpretation of the Bible. Those things, in my view, violate the basic spirit of the gospel and of Jesus.

Q: But they're still part of history, still terrible acts against humanity. Sometimes I even wonder if the world would be better off without religion, or without Christianity, anyway. Is it wrong of me to wonder about that? Maybe it's stupid to wonder about it, since we can never know the answer.

A: You're right, we can never know the answer. But wondering about it is not stupid at all. It's being faithful. There is no getting around the fact that terrible things have been done in the name of Christianity. I think wondering about that is a struggle we need to have because it keeps us a lot more humble than most Christians seem to be. It's a bit like having a lovers' quarrel with institutional Christianity.

But if we can squint beyond those dark times, we would see that there were always Christians who stood against those terrible deeds and who turned Christianity from doing them any more. And we'd also see that the list of good things done by Christians and institutional Christianity is long, too: everything from building schools, colleges, and hospitals; to agencies for helping the poor, the aged, and the orphans; to missions in slums and ghettos and reservations; to inspiring and supporting the arts, music, literature, and poetry; to advocacy for abolition, peacemaking, disarmament, population control, and environment; to ending child labor and sweat shops; to helping people find meaning in their lives and in the universe.

Maybe the balance is only something like sixty percent good to forty percent bad, but if we could quantify it, I'd bet Christianity and its institutions are on the upside of that equation. Any bettors? In any case, God have mercy on us all.

Q: But why does Christianity, at least its organized expression, do things that are quite obviously going to hurt other people, dehumanize them, deeply damage them? Is there something in our religion that makes us do such things?

A: I don't think there's anything in Christianity as a religion, or in its organized forms *per se*, that lends itself to such things. I think destructive things happen when some piece of Scripture gets distorted or taken out of context to justify oppressive action against other people by some vested interest. Slavery, male domination, subjugation of women, oppressive nationalism have all been justified by bits of Scripture interpreted to the advantage of certain factions.

Competing with other religions for followers has also caused the church to take at least some misguided, if not pernicious, positions, and such competition goes on today with similar results, in my view. Also, fear and the desire for certainty seduce us into self-righteous and dogmatic attitudes that demean and discriminate against others.

But I strongly believe that those are distortions of what the gospel is. They are not caused by something in Christianity itself. When any insight, truth, or revelation gets institutionalized, it seems it begins to get corrupted in big way or little ways. My experience is that it happens because the institution becomes more important than the revelation or mission, and the message and mission are put in the service of the institution rather than the other way around. So the church, in order to get along and flourish, recruits members, raises money, builds buildings, supports missions, and so makes accommodations to culture. It backs down from risks and controversy. It becomes dogmatic and inflexible in its adaptations. It becomes as self-serving as other institutions. So Christianity gets distorted.

Q: I think I expect more from the church than that. I expect it to cut through all those sleazy reasons and resist giving in to them. Is that too much to expect?

A: Maybe. But it's not too much to want and work toward. The church is a very human institution with a divine mission, even though we too often trip over our humanity in trying to define and carry out the mission. Reinhold Niebuhr put it well when he said that we ought to be less concerned with the purity of our actions than with the integrity of our compromises. Our *awareness* that our views of God are only sketches, not portraits, helps give integrity to our compromises if we make them in that light and not just for our social success or the status of the institutional church.

Q: How would you define the mission of the church?

A: I think it's what Paul said: to be the body of Christ. That may sound too abstract, so I'd translate the mission as our being disciples, following Jesus, trusting God along with him, joining him in what he did, and what we see he's doing among us now, for justice, peace, healing. The mission isn't to peddle certainty but to promote trust amidst uncertainty; it isn't to seek security but to nurture the love that reduces fear; it isn't to promote perfection but to shrink hypocrisy. It's when we deny our humanity by being self-righteous that we become inhuman. To avoid that, we need to take seriously what Jesus said: ". . . just as you did it [or didn't do it] to one of the least of these who are members of my family, you did it [or didn't do it] to me."[2]

Jesus used the term "family" to include the hungry, the sick, the stranger, the poor, the prisoners—which, one way or another, would pretty much be the whole human family. He talked about an ethic of love, not rules: loving God with all we are, loving our neighbor as our self, loving our enemies. Discerning what it means to love, as God defines love in Jesus, is at the core of the church's mission. Part of the struggle is to figure out that mission as times change, new truth comes to light, and different needs emerge.

Q: So are we back to my question about homosexual persons? Why does the prejudice against them continue to be so strong in the church when the price homosexuals pay in society is so dehumanizing and obvious: all the abuse, violence, and discrimination they deal with?

A: Whatever else it is, that's a prime example of the church's struggle to figure out what it means to love when times change and new information hits the heart and challenges the mind. It's never easy to make those transitions, and it always seems to tax our patience, whichever side of the argument we're on. When our congregation considered years ago becoming a Reconciling Congregation as a stand against our denomination's position that homosexuality was inconsistent with the Christian faith, the church vote was overwhelmingly in favor. But fourteen people voted against it. So, while celebrating the vote,

2. *Matthew 25:40*

we also needed to embrace and love those fourteen people and affirm their importance to us as well. Otherwise our effort to be inclusive would be compromised.

Q: Fourteen out of hundreds isn't many, but the disturbing question is how there can be so many thousands in the church whose view is totally opposed to what others see as obvious?

A: In all fairness, that's the same question those in opposition would ask of those of us who disagree with them. We all have to trust that God will shake it out the right way in time, so we need to keep talking to each other about it. And patiently witnessing to the inclusion our faith compels us toward.

You mentioned the hundreds of years when religion or Christianity called homosexuality sinful or evil. Hundreds of years, or even decades, of believing, thinking, and doing something a certain way makes that way a tradition. Traditions are powerful factors in resisting change. Most pastors can remember coming with new ideas to a church and having people say, "But, Reverend, we always do it this way." That echoes a prominent conservative British noble's words that nothing should ever be done for the first time.

In any case, traditions are not to be taken lightly. Nor are they changed quickly or easily. But the problem is that unexamined tradition or "conventional wisdom" often becomes entrenched as inviolable truth. Yet something becoming conventional doesn't necessarily make it true or right. But when it takes on the authority of the majority, it's risky to challenge it.

Take something like seventeenth-century France, among other places, where it was considered dangerous to take baths because it exposed you to the vapors. That idea lasted a long time. So varieties of perfume were developed and used to cover the smell, and French perfume became the rage. If you thought the vapors might kill you, you'd be reluctant to take a bath. Forget hygiene and just pass the perfume, please. I guess we're indebted to that old bit of conventional wisdom for our variety of perfumes and deodorants.

Q: Isn't it a little weak to compare the lack of French hygiene to the oppression of homosexuals? Oppression is certainly more serious than body odor.

A: It certainly is. But the problem I'm pointing out is that conventional wisdom can be wrong. I think something like that happened with homosexuality. With a couple of exceptions, most cultures shunned or banned homosexuals because no one understood much about them. Certainly where the church had power, there was a simple progression: homosexuals are different, different means unnatural, unnatural means evil, evil means threatening, threatening justifies exclusion and persecution.

That's how conventional wisdom works in lots of areas of life. It gains momentum and rolls down the years. Even today, most people take it as the truth and resist examining it. There are verses in the Old Testament and St. Paul that labeled homosexuals as abominations, and those verses were accepted as God's own condemnation, just as certain passages of the Bible have been used to endorse slavery and oppress women. Jesus said *nothing* about homosexuality, but, in words to take to heart, he warned us not to judge or be judgmental: "For with the judgment you make you will be judged."[3] More people all the time are understanding that homosexuality is a minority sexual orientation—not evil or immoral, and not a threat to the traditional understanding of marriage or our common life.

I believe in twenty years we'll look back and wonder what all the fuss was about. In the meantime, the frustration is that this issue diverts our attention and energy as Christians from outreach in both word and deed. And less attention is given to other critical issues, such as reducing poverty, protecting the environment, developing renewable energy, helping children and low-income families—really, everybody—reducing our consumerism, working with the nations of the world to address the causes of terrorism and tyranny.

3. *Matthew 7:1 ff*

Q: Can't the church take the lead in making inclusion of gay people happen faster?

A: It doesn't look like it. In many ways the rest of society seems to be moving toward inclusion more quickly than the church. Look at television, movies, legislation in Vermont, anti-discrimination rulings by many courts, domestic partner bills in several cities.

I think when we stop dealing with homosexuality as an abstract, generalized issue and start dealing with gay or lesbian persons, giving the issue a human face, seeing homosexual people as people like the rest of us except for their sexual orientation, our attitudes and our actions will change. That's how it happened when our congregation became a Reconciling Congregation. Homosexual persons came out and told their stories. We knew them as faithful, caring, responsible people we loved, and love pins fear to the mat. Isn't that what it means to love: seeing each other as struggling human beings in the same boat?

There are significant numbers of people in the church who are nudging the church in that direction. Twenty years ago, the church wouldn't even be having this discussion. The church can't turn back to those conventional-wisdom days any more than we'll go back to the no-baths, perfume-drenched days. There are no exceptions to the biblical imperative to love, but, obviously and always, there are degrees of difficulty in application. So our struggles will be ongoing.

Q: But gay marriage is a hot topic, a big battle right now. There's even a movement to make a constitutional amendment to ban it. What about that?

A: Oh my, that question is so loaded emotionally. But I think the issue at stake is a deeper one. Who defines marriage? I don't think any church should define marriage for everyone. Yet, over time, the authority for doing that apparently has fallen to the church. Social expectations, not religious considerations, often pressure people to be married in the church when they have no particular interest in Christianity or don't intend to ever darken the sanctuary doors again. Any religious implications are really superfluous. That's a sham and involves us in the hypocrisy of which Jesus was most critical. And it puts ministers in the position of performing weddings not only as clerical representatives of the church but also as legal representatives of the state. I don't think the church or clergy should act as agents of the state in performing marriages.

The state should not legally discriminate between citizens based on their religion, race, gender, sexual orientation, or political affiliation. Nor do I believe the church and clergy should support the state or nation in making constitutional amendments to discriminate against anyone, including gays and lesbians and their equal rights under the law. My problem with marriage for same sex persons is the same as with marriage for different sex persons: the linking of church and state in defining who can or can't be legally married.

Q: But isn't that linking permanent? How could it ever be changed?

A: Permanent is a long time, and not much qualifies for that status. I think any change depends on people being concerned about the separation of church and state, and recognizing the danger to both in any institutional overlapping. It seems to me that the First Amendment about separation of church and state doesn't change the responsibility of the state to apply laws fairly and equally to all persons and institutions, on one hand. And on the other hand, it doesn't change the right of the church to challenge the state to act to remedy unjust or oppressive conditions that dehumanize people. The amendment distinguishes between the two, and so separates them and their responsibilities and powers.

Q: So what is your proposal concerning this issue?

A: My view is that marriage as a *legal status* is the province of the state, and marriage as a *religious covenant* is the province of religious institutions. It is similar to the practice of those countries where people have a civil marriage for legal purposes and an optional church, synagogue, or mosque service if they want marriage to be a religious covenant. For the civil marriage, the couple has to meet legal requirements of the state, which protects all people legally, as it does anyone making a legal contract. For a religious or church service, they need only to meet the requirements of the church, which doesn't change the legal status of their civil marriage.

I would advocate for that process to be adopted in this country. The state should set the legal definition of marriage but not have the right to tell the church who it can marry in a religious service. Nor should the church determine who is eligible for a legal marriage.

At the same time, the church has the right to decide who they will marry in a religious service, and different churches would make different judgments about that, but this would give people some choices among churches with differing positions on the issue.

In addition, I simply don't agree with those who believe gay marriage threatens the status of marriage and family in this society. Infidelity, spouse abuse, child abuse, poverty, casual divorce, lack of child support, deficient pre-marital counseling, inadequate education, poor schools—*those* are threatening to the stability of marriage, not the love and commitment of two people of homosexual orientation.

Q: What is the purpose of celebrating a marriage in the church, from the church's point of view?

A: It's to sanctify or bless the covenant of the two people in the sight of God and to confirm it in the community of faith. A covenant has an extra dimension beyond the legal contract.

It defines what commitment means, what trust requires, what fidelity involves, what real intimacy entails, what limitations mean, what love includes, how faith deepens.

In the Christian context of covenant, I am not asking or expecting my partner to mean everything to me, nor am I expecting to mean everything to my partner. No person can be for another what only God can be. That truth is part of that extra-legal dimension to marriage as a religious covenant. It also includes the community of faith to support us and hold us accountable in the process of being married.

Q: But just because people can get legally married in other places than church doesn't change the fact that marriage is a covenant, and all that a covenant means, does it?

A: No, not necessarily. Certainly not if the religious nature of the service is taken seriously by the people being married. But having to get a license from the state for a marriage service in a religious institution certainly muddies the water between church and state, and between marriage as a legal status and marriage as a religious covenant. Once the state discriminates against a minority for supposedly "religious" reasons, such as being homosexual, the door is open to discriminating against people for other supposed religious reasons, such as belonging to the "wrong" religion, or for being unbelievers, or not believing in the "right" religion in the "right" way. You can imagine where that leads.

Conversely, if the state tells the church who it can marry, religious belief and practice gets shaped by the law of the state, which is as pernicious as shaping state laws by religious doctrine. Either way, we move toward theocracy, a society of a single religious position imposed on everyone. History, including recent history, shows that theocracy can oppress and damage millions of people in the name of God.

Q: But don't we call ourselves a "Christian nation"?

A: Even if we did call ourselves a "Christian nation," which many don't, it would be hard to know what is meant by that term. For one thing, it implies a unanimous view of what it means to be Christian, which obviously there isn't. It also implies a very questionable claim of a higher moral rectitude and authority than other nations. Reinhold Niebuhr's realism about that has it right. Essentially his view is that we're just bad enough to make democracy necessary and just good enough to make it work.

Our nation certainly includes a majority of people of faith. The founders of our country had religious and philosophical orientations toward God but not an official church. They definitely rejected that option. They knew that once religion becomes institutionalized by the state, both begin to die.

As much as some people insist we're a "Christian nation," or should be, that would preclude the importance of other religions and philosophies to our country in the past as well as now and in the future. I am a committed Christian, but I am not an advocate of the religious rule or a theocracy, such as Afghanistan had with such oppressive consequences for women and others. I don't believe in a state religion or a religious state, as such. Frankly, I believe God works better through dynamic diversity than through the uniformity of a static institution or the divine right of kings, presidents, or bishops, or anyone claiming to know God's mind.

Q: As you talk, I've been thinking about the California atheist who sued to take the words "under God" out of the Pledge of Allegiance because those words imply state-ordained religious instruction. In some ways it seems a trivial issue, but it isn't so trivial, is it?

A: Why do you think it isn't?

Q: Because the "under God" part was added in the fifties to highlight that we're the "good guys" and godless communists were the "bad guys." Isn't that more a political statement than a religious one? Isn't it dangerous to make religion serve government's purposes?

A: I agree. And yet the issue is a bit of an emotional Catch-22 for me. Part of me thinks, "What's so wrong with saying 'under God'"? After all, we aren't saying what kind of God we're under, so it isn't indoctrination of a particular religion. Those words can mean any kind of God—but I don't think I really want to go there. It's a little like bumper stickers that say, and politicians who end their speeches saying, "God bless America." I wish we said, and meant, "God bless America and the world," and then added, "Bless them through us."

Q: I thought you were going to say that our nation doesn't act as if it's under God. Is that what you mean?

A: No, not really. But whether we act like it or not, we know at some point or other that history will roll over us because it isn't just America that God cares about or blesses, or works to redeem. It's so easy to misconstrue that our beloved country is acting "under God" or is blessed by God just because we're glad to be Americans. Not long ago a national leader publicly said that if a sparrow can't fall without God's knowledge, surely an empire can't rise without God's support. And that's wrong! Did God support the Roman Empire, the Ottoman Empire, or the Nazi Third Reich? Surely not! We really do have to learn that "God 'n' country" are *not* one word, as Bill Coffin puts it.

After I'd been at FUMCOG[4] a while, I talked to people and we decided to take the American flag out of the sanctuary and put it in another part of the building. That didn't mean we loved our country any less, or weren't grateful for it and to it, or weren't responsible for our actions as citizens. But the flag isn't a Christian

4. *First United Methodist Church of Germantown, Philadelphia*

symbol and doesn't belong in worship. Protecting the separation of church and state is hard but necessary for both.

One last comment here. I believe we should not leave any area of life out of our faith orientation. Our Christian faith is about our integrity before God, not the enforcement of our views and positions on others. As Protestant Christians, our faith involves a continuing reformation. That reformation requires dialogue with others about what the kingdom of God means to and for us, what Jesus is calling us to be and do in loving God and neighbor and enemy. It includes incorporating new experiences, being open to new thoughts, expanding our ethical and spiritual imagination, being constantly accountable. Conformity, arrogance, and domination just don't wash.

Q: Don't you agree that when we say "under God" as part of the Pledge of Allegiance, it's like asking God to take care of us because God's on our side, not on other guys' side?

A: That's certainly one interpretation. But the whole thing is a little dicey because there are so many possible ways to hear it. Maybe "under God" expresses a hope. If it's a claim, it's too parochial. It's a little like the debate about whether prayer should be allowed in the public schools. Anybody who thinks there's no prayer in public schools has never taken an exam there! Or taught there. It's just not official or imposed. We don't have to *say* "under God" to believe it's true for all countries, ultimately.

Q: I want to go back a minute to what you were saying about marriage. You used words like sanctify, covenant, blessing. What do you mean by those words?

A: Those words refer to another world, another dimension, consistently filtering into and through this one. They refer to another reality pervading the reality we think is all there is to life. Words such as sanctify, bless, redeem, heal, reveal, and reconcile all point to that other reality. So does the word kingdom, and certainly the Spirit of God. Those words touch on the deeper meaning of life itself.

Think of taking an oath as a witness in court. You put your hand on a Bible and swear "to tell the truth, the whole truth, and nothing but the truth." While you realize that you don't know, and so can't tell, the whole truth—or even nothing but the truth—still, if you understand the oath as being made before God, you will stick to the truth you do know because you are responsible to a greater power than just self-interest, avoiding perjury, or court judgments. Truth is rooted in the heart, not just the mind. Truth is connected to what it means to love God, self, and neighbor, and it leads to living by the covenant of justice, healing, reconciliation among us, no matter who, where, or what we are.

Q: My son, Josh, is getting married in July. I've been having something like this very conversation with him. We have different perspectives, and we're learning from each other. He asks why he should have a religious service when so much of the church seems irrelevant and hypocritical. I am willing to trust that there is a Being who blesses us even when we don't acknowledge it. . . . Can you find a question in there somewhere?

A: At least there's no question that human relationships in any form are really complicated! It sounds as if you and Josh have gotten closer and more trusting with each other through sharing your differences. You deserve credit for that.

As I hear it, your question has to do with marriage as a covenant, not just a legal contract with legal protections for the couple and their kids. You want marriage to mean more than a contract to Josh, and you wonder if it can mean more than that if the wedding isn't overtly religious.

For most people, I think marriage is more than just a legal arrangement, even if they don't consciously think of themselves as religious. We all sense that there is something inherently sacred about human relationships and human beings. We're hardwired that way—until some of us get short-circuited by something.

A church wedding makes public the sacredness of human relationships and roots the sacredness in God. *Covenant* is a religious term that means something more profound than we can fully grasp. By the grace of God, the covenant between us and God ultimately can't be broken. In some ways, neither can the covenant with each other in marriage, or in society, because that relationship becomes part of who we are—even after it is evidently and legally ended. But neither party to a human covenant is God, so marriage is not inviolable, not in the face of dehumanizing circumstances. It's similar to what Jesus said about the Sabbath: "The sabbath was made for humankind, and not humankind for the sabbath."[5]

Marriage is sacred but not unconditional. When I was divorced, I was extremely anguished by breaking something that was more than a legal contract. I think most people feel that anguish if they divorce. Divorce violates something sacred between two people, even if some wouldn't describe it that way. Usually it takes a severely painful situation to end a marriage. In my case the anguish was magnified because, as a minister, the divorce was not only a family crisis but a public ordeal. People in the congregation, in the larger church, in the community, were very upset because I was doing something contrary to their expectations of ministers.

Q: But that came out all right, didn't it?

A: Probably *mostly* right, not *all* right. We were hurt. Family was hurt. People were hurt. At times through the process, I was despondent. The congregation had to consider whether to ask me to leave. The church authorities had to consider whether to rescind my ordination. It was hard not to just walk away.

The reason I didn't is because I wanted to fight those options. The church isn't meant to be like a company that gives you insurance only if you prove you don't need it, or that gathers only those whose sins are more like a hair in the

5. *Mark 2:27*

mouth than an abscessed tooth. That encourages superficiality and makes forgiveness trivial.

The congregation managed to push through their hurt and fear to some deeper level of forgiveness and healing, and to some realization that being untainted isn't a requirement for either the clergy or the laity. The church is for all of us, and any of us. So we can be done with pretense and be with each other, honestly holding each other accountable while supporting each other in humility, love, mercy, challenge, and growth. Then, by God's grace, we can become what I think the body of Christ should be, in and through us, for the world.

Q: If covenants, like marriage, get broken pretty easily and often, doesn't that mean they aren't taken very seriously in the first place and don't matter that much? And moral dictates as well?

A: No and *no*! I don't mean to suggest that in the slightest. Covenants matter hugely, as does morality. Things that relate to justice, peace, and reconciliation matter enormously. The issue is that everyone doesn't agree on how or what to do about those things.

So it isn't that morality and covenants don't matter, because they do. The rub is that they don't matter so much that any particular version of them can or should be made absolute and enforced in any and all circumstances. That's one of the major conflicts of our culture right now between (A) those who insist there are absolute moral or religious truths that apply to all situations, and (B) those who insist these truths, however "absolute," don't always—perhaps ever—apply specifically in every situation. In fact, "B people" insist we can't know those absolute truths so absolutely and clearly as to rigidly apply them in human affairs, and we leave those absolutes to God. So we get called "relativists," which in a way we are, because God makes love an absolute moral position but doesn't give us details about what love means in every situation or choice.

"The truth" is less what we have than "a truth," and in dialogue with others about "their truths" and "our truths," both can become larger and deeper. We may not like that process because to enter it we need to confess that "our truths" are always limited, however firm and deeply rooted we believe they are. But that's what it means to respond to the kingdom of God, among us or between us. That what it means to trust that God's grace overrides all our little truths so we can hold them less tightly and be open to others less defensively, though still thoughtfully and critically.

We need to keep aware that religion or faith is finally not about us. It's about God and what kind of God we believe in. It's not preoccupation with "Do I measure up? Am I absolutely right or pure?" Because if that's what it is, the game is over very quickly. But it's not. It's what Paul said, and we keep hanging on to: ". . . neither death, nor life, nor angels, nor rulers, nor things present, nor things to come . . . nor anything else in all creation, will be able to separate us from the love of God in Christ Jesus our Lord."[6] That makes life, faith, and the world a whole different matter.

In my view, the Christian understanding of covenant is that God keeps the covenant even when we break it. And in reality, we break it before breakfast because by then we have not loved God with all our heart and with all our soul and strength and our neighbor as ourselves. So we are literally saved by grace, not by virtue. That is not to be taken for granted or abused but understood as the freedom to keep trying as best we can to love where we are. Of course, ". . . all we like sheep have gone astray . . ." but that isn't to say we go astray or stay astray as if it didn't matter. We realize that our going astray means that the shepherd has to leave the ninety-nine at some risk in order to come and get us back on track. Which means, back where we can help the shepherd take care of the ninety-nine and even go with God after the "one's" in our neck of the brambles and wilderness.

6. *Romans 8:38-39*

Q: What happens if we really invest in covenant, be it marriage or church membership, or things we take with great heart, and then it all changes. Does that mean we've gone astray if we re-evaluate things and make a different choice? After years of an empty marriage, and lots of marital counseling, I got divorced, but I still parent our kids with my former husband. Now I'm struggling with my church, which has changed so much from what I think the church should be, and yet neither leaving or staying seems authentic or honest. I don't leave, but I don't go to church either. Am I one of the ninety-nine or am I the one who has gone astray?

A: I believe we're all among the ninety-nine, as well as being the lost one. Each of the ninety-nine is also the "one" in their own way. Because we're the one, we can help God find the other ninety-nine one's because we know where to look for them. We've been there, done that, may even still be there doing that. Knowing you're one *out* of a hundred and yet one *in* ninety-nine is part of the mysterious paradox of faith and of grace.

Luther's words help me with this: "Trust God and sin on boldly," a variation on what Augustine said earlier, "Love God and do as you please." I think they're both referring to the freedom not to be so afraid we can't move. I think there's a liberating difference between trusting God and sinning on boldly, and just going on boldly in something like stoic cynicism. The "sinning on boldly" is a radical risk of faith. It's trusting God that since we are going to sin even while doing good things, we can go on in the confidence that it isn't going to be the end of the world for us or for God or for other people. New things will still become possible by the grace of God, who is always making all things new both through us and in spite of us.

That doesn't mean we can be careless about what we're doing. It's a way of saying, again with Luther, "Here I stand . . ." or "Here I walk without fainting" but by faith, not by sight.

To acknowledge that God is always part of our lives and world is not to say that we're certain of all God is or what God will do in any complete or final way. No one knows that. But

I choose to trust without knowing because the mystery of God is God's freedom to be God in the way God is God, not the way I want God to be God, or the way I think God has to be God. There is an impassable divide between God and us.

Q: But if the gap is impassable, doesn't that mean we really can't know anything at all about God, or even that there is one? That pretty much knocks the props out from under religion, doesn't it?

A: That the gap is impassable from our side doesn't mean it is from God's side. God shows us enough, in enough different ways, for us to affirm some things, albeit different things, about God. We hold in common that there are certain characteristics that apply to God—for instance, that God is eternal, powerful, wise, righteous, just, merciful, holy.

But the variations of what those characteristics mean, how they apply in specific human life and history, are so many that none of us can claim that we know God absolutely. It's ironic that for scientists, physicists, and astronomers, mysteries and uncertainties are essential to their work, while religionists and preachers, even some theologians, deal in absolutes and infallibility in talking of God. For me, that's a disastrous, tyrannous overreach. It's a Babel complex. Bricks are useful, helpful, and so are beliefs, but not to climb out of our humanity and achieve divinity.

Q: So where does that leave us in this world? In a pretty shaky position, doesn't it?

A: It leaves us with faith, trust, and living out our beliefs with humility. If humility is what shaky means, then, yes, it leaves us in that position. And yet grace means we're shaky on a firm foundation, to borrow an image from an old hymn. That makes it a good shaky.

In my judgment, humility is lacking in the public discussion, whether it's about religion, politics, morality, or social issues. We all prefer certainty to truth. It doesn't seem to matter what the truth might be, we just want to be certain. That's why political leaders can literally "spin" truth, or distort factual information, and we'll accept it as long as they smile and figuratively flex their muscles to assure us. And that's one of the reasons why fundamentalism appeals to people: Believe this, do this, and you're saved for sure. There's a real appeal in such certainty, even if we have to turn off our God-given minds to get it, or turn against our own conscience or heart.

Q: So that's the human dilemma? Having to gamble between false certainty and shaky faith?

A: Sort of. But remember I said there is a firm foundation under a shaky faith. It's pointed to in the Bible and in the life, death, and resurrection of Jesus—and in the church, at its best. Holding our shaky faith together with others gives it a more firm foundation. That can help make the world a little less shaky.

The point I'm trying to get to here is that there's a certain freedom in not having to be right. There's a certain freedom in not worrying whether your stand, or what you're doing at every point, is absolutely right, good, and true. What is asked of us is to accept our humanity, to be and do as much right, good, and truth as we can at any given moment, and to admit that we don't know the outcome of it all. It's like giving whatever loaves and fishes we have and realizing there could be good leftovers we didn't expect. Or bad ones we need to be forgiven for. In other words, what is good and right and true may all be changed by God or circumstance. And we may change, please God. Hopefully that's part of the process, part of the excitement of walking by faith, of becoming wise, or growing in relationships or love or whatever.

I don't think it's helpful to encounter changed circumstances and respond by hanging on to some comfortable but mistaken view we insist is true. I don't see my job, or that of Christians, to go out and try to force the world into THE truth. It's a dead end to get locked into an idolatry with no options, no choices. Rather my job, our job as Christians, is to go out into the world with our shaky faith and live by a process by which our truth and the truth of others interact to heal, do justice, bless the world, and create more chances for God to work and the kingdom to come.

Q: When I got divorced, I think the hardest thing wasn't so much that the relationship was ended, but that the pledge I had made to something bigger than me had been broken. I'm not sure I've ever gotten over that. I went to leaders and people in the church we belonged to and told them what was happening and asked them to love us and to do the best they could to support us. But afterward, phone calls weren't returned, people avoided me. It made me feel as if words like covenant are worth little or nothing. So when you try to live by a shaky faith with a firm foundation, or however you put it, it can get real messy.

A: Yes, it can.

Q: Then what can I do?

A: I think you know the only answer there really is to that. You live in and through the mess. That's what Jesus did all the time. You're a walking resurrection of sorts. After all, here you are, with a wife who adores you, a daughter who did not abandon you when you and her mother divorced but stood by you both, and accepts and loves you both. And you are surrounded by friends who love and support and are grateful for you.

Put it this way. Any covenant that we make together is an echo or reflection of the covenant with God. As I said earlier, God keeps that covenant in place in spite of the fact that we break it over and over and over. Your life is a confirmation of that. Plus, you don't know what kind of little shift those people in the church might have experienced because you spoke to them and asked them to support you. Maybe they'll do that for the next person.

When I was going through my divorce, I got letters saying, "If this can happen to you, it can happen to me." There's a redeeming self-awareness in the writers of those letters. My situation was a wake-up call for them. It opened them up in a different way to be different people than they might have been otherwise in their marriages, families, all around. I think that's how God works among us.

There's a saying that has meant a lot to me: "A broken heart can contain the whole universe." It means a lot to me because I break people's hearts. They break my heart. We break each other's hearts, in and out of marriage. We break our own hearts, we break our children's hearts by breaking their expectations of us, the expectations we set them up to have. But, by the grace of God, a broken heart can contain the whole world, the whole universe. When our hearts break, we can either become cynical and bitter and judgmental, or we can step out on the promise and become newly open to God, grateful for the world, compassionate and embracing of other people because they are just like us in their broken hearts.

Let's admit that saying other people are "just like us" can be offensive because it fails to draw a line between us and killers, rapists, terrorists, all sorts of sick, corrupted people. But we also have to ask if those people are really so terribly different from us? Different, yes. But terribly so? I don't know about you, but I've had impulses to kill somebody when I've been enraged or frustrated or scared or whatever. And yes, there are people with all kinds of destructive delusions, paranoias, pathologies, anxieties, or depressions. But having been in extensive therapy myself, I understand a little more about that, about us all, than I would otherwise, and I realize I'm not one-hundred-eighty degrees different from "them"—or anyone else.

So, our hearts break. The world isn't perfect. *We're* not perfect. But in the breaking, something else happens. That's the mystery of God. That's the mystery of grace. It isn't that next time we'll be better, but it may be that next time we'll be more faithful. Next time we'll be wiser. Next time we'll be more compassionate. Next time winning and being right won't matter quite as much. Next time our heart will contain more of the kingdom.

When I made the connection that in the breakup of my marriage I was as much at fault as she was, new possibilities for love and change came from that awareness. I pray that my broken heart will contain the whole universe with more wonder, gratitude, tenderness, and fidelity.

Q: As you talk about this, I think about how in my own mind I get anxious: "Am I doing the right thing? Am I good? Is what I'm doing the best response to a bad situation?" But, in fact, the whole situation reflects a brokenness that's part of me, and that I'm part of, and that everybody is connected to. It's knowing that I can trust God is at work in that bigger underlying brokenness, even through me, that is such a gift. It is so liberating. So integrating. Thanks for helping me with that.

A: That's a very profound, faithful response to a holy process. I'm glad if we helped.

Q: I'm pretty sure you did.

A: Thanks. God sure did. I guess that's quite enough for this time. Go well and stay watchful.

Fourth Sharing

O God, here we are, our spirits bereft, our minds grasping for answers beyond those that do not yet persuade, our hearts aching with sadness, anger, and fears. We seek some refuge under the shadow of your wings. Comfort us as a mother comforts her children. Hear our tears as prayers, our ache as longing. Ease our anger and hush our fears. Shepherd us through this wilderness and bring us closer to you and to each other. Let your Spirit be as breath to Celeste and her family as they cope with the loss of Sherwood. Enable them to wait upon you that they may walk and not faint because you walk with them. Amen.

All of us are in shock and grief over the news that Celeste's son, Sherwood, was killed in Iraq last week. His death is a blow to us all, but most of all to Celeste and Al, who remain close though divorced, and to their sons, Dante and Raphael. We all have a tangle of feelings for them—and about the Iraq war and Sherwood being killed and all the other soldiers and all the Iraqi people killed, all the children, and everything.

The thing is, the "everything" of it really comes down to the loss of a human being and what that means to his family and friends, the loss of Sherwood and every other person killed in this ugly war, both Americans and Iraqis. That's the core truth of it, and we need to keep that in focus in whatever other directions and issues we connect with Sherwood's death. I trust we will all pray for Celeste, Al, Dante, and Raphael in the days ahead. And pray, as well, for all the families of our country and Iraq who are involved in this war. And pray for peace.

This loss, this grief, will remain as a presence among us. It's on our minds and hearts, and we will carry it a very long time. I believe it's on God's mind and heart, too, as is Sherwood, and from that we can draw comfort and strength. I believe that whatever we do to respond to the loss of Sherwood and to be with the Zapalla family is connected to the community of faith that they and we are part of. It all has to do with the value of each one of us to God and to each other—and not taking anything for granted. It's about making our stands and our witnesses about things we believe in, and at the same time not losing track of one another in that process. It means turning away from the tyranny of ideology and turning toward the compassion of faith.

If anyone wants to add something, please do. Then let's have a few minutes of silent prayer during which you can pray aloud if you are so moved.

Q 1: I appreciate your comments. Sherwood and the family are heavy on my heart. It would feel crazy not to acknowledge that.

Q 2: I'm struck by what you said, but also by what no one can say yet about Sherwood's death and the family's grief. This war is so disorienting to everyone. It's making us all crazy.

A: I agree. Any attempt tonight to dissect that issue, or any part of it, is not the place to start, and it's not the place to stop. We start with some kind of faith orientation, and we go on from there. That is what is sustaining and what we share.

Q 2: I was glad for the silent prayer time, but I think we need someone to pray out loud to help us focus. Would you be willing to do that now? It would help us feel more connected.

A: Sure. Let's hold hands and pray together.

O God, here we are, struggling to be faithful and groping to find our way. We're shaken and disoriented by events in Iraq, and now Sherwood's death and the storm of grief and loss and anger it stirs up in his family's hearts and home. Lord, steady them with your comfort and be the North Star in their darkness. Hold Sherwood close to your heart as we lift him to you from ours. Hold us all as well and bring out of this, and out of us, something saving and sustaining. We trust you hear the prayers we mean as well as those we say, for we pray in Jesus' name. Amen.

Did anybody come with a question?

Q 1: Sherwood's death makes me think about what might happen after death, and what resurrection is about. Earlier you said that we would be resurrected not as a literal body but as a "person" who would be a particular presence or recognizable individual beyond death. I had never heard it quite that way before. I think we ended the discussion before it was over. Could you say more about that now, or is this not a good time?

A: Under the circumstances, it's probably a good time.

Q 2: As I recall a previous discussion, you talked about Jesus' resurrection in an unconventional but fascinating way that made sense. You said it wasn't Jesus' body, necessarily, that was there with the women and disciples, but that they felt his presence and that was enough. They told others it was his body to convey the connection they felt.

A: Let me say first off that I didn't mean to suggest in any way that the resurrection meant that the disciples just "felt" Jesus' presence. That's too vague and invites interpreting the event as some kind of psychological phenomenon produced by distraught or guilty people.

That's not what the Gospels say about the disciples' experiences of Jesus' resurrection.

Until quite recently the Greek division of mind-body-spirit has been part of our Western thought processes. On the other hand, the Jews understand the mind, body, spirit as being different functions of one whole, indivisible person. When you look at the Gospel versions of resurrection from a Jewish perspective, it leads to a different interpretation than the Greek perspective does. Jesus' resurrection, and any other resurrection, means that the mind and spirit are resurrected by God as a gift and given a new but recognizable body. We all know what it means to say that a person's face reflects his or her spirit, that their life is written in their face, hands, eyes, walk, voice. I think the meaning of the resurrection of the body lies in that direction, not in a literal interpretation. And that view isn't very innovative; it's more traditional.

Q 1: Can you go further explaining that?

A: Only if you'll keep in mind that you're right in saying that, in our last discussion of this, we stopped before it was over. That's always the case when we're talking about "after death," since we can't really know this side of the veil. I think Jesus' promise that he was going to prepare a place for us is as far as we can go into that unknown territory—and it's far enough, isn't it?

I don't doubt the larger truth of what Paul said when he described being taken up into heaven and hearing things no mortal can repeat.[1] Or John's beautiful words written out there on Patmos surrounded by the sea, words we've heard at many funerals, poetic images of a new heaven and a new earth, visions of God wiping away all tears from mortals' eyes and death being no more.[2] But even those two biblical writers were careful not to transgress on the mystery and used poetic images to point to truths beyond what words could wholly capture.

1. *2 Corinthians 12:2-4*
2. *Revelation 21:1, 4*

Q: Are you saying that we can't really know much about what comes after death? What's the point of trying then?

A: I suppose a better word than "know" here is "discern." We can discern a few things about what comes after death from what the Bible says about it, and from our own deep longing for those we've loved and lost. Our longing for life beyond death seems hardwired into us. A death in the "family" intensifies that longing, as Sherwood's does.

Q: But we don't get everything we long for, do we?

A: We all know the answer is "No." So the first measure for discerning anything about life after death starts with the kind of God we see in Jesus, not with ourselves or our feelings and thoughts. What we say or believe about life after death is rooted in what Jesus said and showed us about God.

A close, deeply Christian friend of mine, then in his mid-seventies, said to me that he didn't believe in life after death anymore because one life was gift enough. I asked him what about kids who die in infancy or are born with terrible deformities or awful retardation. What about young people who die in wars or accidents, or suffer incurable diseases? What kind of God would leave those lives so painfully unfulfilled and not resurrect them to something else? Such a God would be less moral, less loving than Jesus. My friend allowed that was something he hadn't thought about.

Q: Do you think that changed his mind?

A: Just unsettled it a little, which was the point. I asked my friend why did Jesus talk of there being more than just death at the end of life, even one badly lived. I told him that, if he were at all like me, he surely had unfulfilled longings for his life. So I asked if our lives as humans wouldn't be an awful waste if, having come out of the Big Bang all the way to being thinking, feeling, self-conscious, and universe-conscious beings, with such capacity to be moral and loving, God would then let us just be snuffed out. What kind of God would that be? He said he had to consider that but still felt that concern for life after death was selfish.

Q: But aren't there are a lot of people who think that about human beings, that we are like everything else that withers and dies?

A: Sure. Some part of all of us struggles with that possibility, too. That struggle is part of our grieving and fear.

Some religious leaders tried to push Jesus about resurrection by asking him whose wife a childless widow would be in the resurrection if, as required by Jewish law, each of the dead husband's seven brothers in turn, had married her when their preceding brother died. Jesus reminded them that God was ". . . the God of Abraham, the God of Isaac, and the God of Jacob." then added "He is God not of the dead, but of the living."[3] Jesus was saying that though Abraham, Isaac, and Jacob had been considered to have been long dead, they were still alive in the God of the living. Life after death is about God.

To forget that makes us go off in fruitless, if not faithless, directions—such as whether resurrection of the body means we shouldn't be cremated, or whether we're going to be resurrected as eighteen- or eighty-year-olds, or be raised as hunks or chunks or whatever.

One other thing I discern is that we'll have a body that bears Jesus' healing touch yet is shaped by our own spirit, mind, heart, and personal life experience. A body, in the Jewish sense of a person, carries the continuity between the "then," and the "now," and the "next." So I believe the resurrection of the body carries the continuity through time and eternity.

Q: And that's what you think, or discern, happened when Jesus was resurrected? I always thought Jesus appeared in his real, physical body. You make it sound different, less miraculous.

3. *Matthew 22:32*

A: I don't in any way mean to suggest or imply that Jesus' body wasn't real or even physical in some dimension. Who he was, or is, after his death is a continuation in a recognizable form of who he was in his time on earth. The disciples and women recognized him not only as a person they'd known but as a relationship they'd had. That *double* recognition is the key element of the resurrection. When Jesus first appeared to the disciples, they thought he was a ghost until he showed them the nail wounds in his hands and feet. He wasn't an unreal apparition but a deeper reality than they had ever known.

Jesus' resurrection sent them into the world on a mission that was dangerous but exciting and life-giving. They weren't afraid to go, even if it killed them. And it did, some of them anyway. A guilt-driven psychological phenomenon wouldn't have done that nor would a vague spiritual moment. Only the deeper reality opened to them by this resurrected person they knew before his death could do that. They came late to trust him after the resurrection. That made them less afraid of death, or defeat, or any other disaster.

Now here we are struggling with the loss of Sherwood, and death breaks in on us full force again. And so does resurrection.

Q: Do you think our resurrection is the same as going to heaven?

A: Now you're being really pushy! I don't know. Maybe not so radically different. A few years ago, I read Jeffery Burton Russell's book *A History of Heaven.* When I finished, the mystery was as deep as ever, despite all the research on historical views of heaven. But I do remember two or three things the author said. One was that humans are their most real in heaven. Another was that heaven is the silence singing. And another was that heaven is where God is. I think all those notions are provocative but especially the last one. That one's enough for me. I hope it's enough for you, too. And for Sherwood.

Q: Doesn't the resurrection mean we've got to be transformed some way? There's got to be some major difference between this life and the next one, doesn't there?

A: Yes, of course. That's why we say those stupendous words of John at the funerals of our loved ones as we commit them to God: "Death will be no more . . . And there will be no more night . . . for the Lord God will be their light."⁴ That's a huge difference, isn't it?

But I don't believe resurrection and life after death means we're made perfect in a blink so it's all over but the shouting, or the singing, or whatever. I hold that whatever heaven or resurrection turn out to be for us, we will still have the limitations of creaturely life. We will not be God. We'll be creatures—not self-created beings but dependent beings. If nothing else, just by being raised to live again, we get more chances to change and grow.

Q: What do you mean "more chances"?

A: Every day of our lives we get up with more chances to do something different from what we did the day before. More chances to love more, or make amends, or reach out, or create, or challenge, or speak, or whatever it is we have a chance to do.

Well, I'm assuming that after death, when we "get up in the morning" we will have more chances as well, maybe on a different scale, but still chances to grow in love, peace, justice, beauty, joy, and wisdom, and in all the things and ways we know are incomplete in us, and because of us, now.

John Wesley said there's no such thing as a solitary Christian. Well, there's no such thing as a solitary human being, either. We become human together. So in our resurrected state, I believe we'll relate and become more deeply, fully human together. Become more like Jesus, more like God created us to be. I, for one, can't do that by myself *now*, so how could I do

4. *Revelation 21:4; 22:5*

it alone *then*? I need people to mutually challenge, confront, chip away at my ME-ism. The love that I've been given by other people, and tried to give back, the living deeper and deeper by being crunched and re-crunched and re-constituted and recycled, as it were—those are the things that have mattered to me here and now, and will then and there. That's what I mean by more chances. But no matter what self-appointed gate keepers may say to the contrary, I believe there are going to be a lot of surprises among resurrected persons in heaven, thank God!

Q: Do you think the development, or the continuation, of Christianity was dependent upon Christ being resurrected in some form?

A: It seems to me that's the case . . . as long as the resurrection includes everything Jesus was, did, thought. That holistic view of Jesus and resurrection moves it all past the realm of a philosophical or ethical thinking. It points to a person who didn't just teach ideas about God but actually demonstrated the historical reality of them *and* their eternal significance.

Here's why so much rides on that: Death is the unavoidable block in the road of humanity. We can't get around it. By death I mean, first off, the final one that smells of the void and annihilation. But I also mean all the little deaths along the way. They ripple toward us from that final one, somehow: the fear, the sense of despair and impotence, the misplaced loyalties, the rage, the violence. Death refers us to God and whether there is one or not, to what God is like and whether death trumps everything.

There are many philosophical arguments for and against the existence of God, and for and against life after death. Many are good. Like Immanuel Kant saying that there are two things that inspire awe: "the starry heavens without and the moral law within." He says that the fulfillment of that inward law will take life beyond the grave. That seems to make a philosophical case for God and for life after death. But I have to say, even though it's not fair to that great philosopher, philosophical arguments are like bubble-less champagne: They don't buzz the heart.

There are many intriguing myths about God and death, as Joseph Campbell walked us through in his television interviews and in his books. Like the creation stories in Genesis, myths often point powerfully to profound truths. But they seem to tell us more about our selves, our needs—and our visions and ingenuity in meeting them—than about some Other, who breaks in on us, confronts and claims us, and adds another dimension to our historical reality. That isn't to devalue myths, but I'm being simplistic to make a point.

When it is rooted in historical origins, religion goes beyond philosophy and myth. It isn't so much about what someone thought but about what happened and what the happening means. Jesus' resurrection gathered up who he was and turned the disciples around. Christianity has to do with the *way* they got turned around, and *by whom*. Christianity wasn't an idea. It wasn't a good marketing device. It was about something, or Someone, happening that made people change their lives and share them with others in a compelling way. Jesus is the intersect of mystery and history.

Q: Could I ask you a historical question about that time?

A: Well, I wasn't alive then, but go ahead.

Q: Right. Anyway, after the crucifixion and the resurrection, how much time was there during which there wasn't really a movement following Jesus? I have trouble sorting it out, but I have the impression that the Gospels were written some significant time after Jesus' life.

A: Paul's letters were the earliest writings in what we call the New Testament. Scholars think Mark is the earliest Gospel to be written, and that was about forty years after Jesus' life.

Q: Doesn't that mean there was a period after the crucifixion when there wasn't a "Jesus movement"? Could it be that the resurrection appearances happened not right after the crucifixion but long after that? Could it be that, by then, the references to the resurrected body were actually about the church as the body of Christ? If that's what the bodily appearances might refer to, then we could put aside agonizing over the physical details of Jesus' resurrection in the Gospels.

A: Did you stay awake nights thinking that one up? It's true that the church, as the body of Christ, is called to *reflect* the resurrection, but not to *be* the resurrection. Besides, there really was what you call a "Jesus movement" shortly after he died and was resurrected. Actually, the only thing Jesus left was that little company of people, the church. He left no autobiography except what was written in the lives and experiences of the disciples, and that included his resurrection.

It was that little body of people of faith who had been with him who kept the stories of Jesus alive in an oral tradition. It took time for them to realize they should start writing down the stories. They hadn't done that before because they probably thought Jesus would be coming back any minute. Eschatology was embedded in the early church, replete with claims about Jesus' imminent coming again to establish the kingdom of God on earth. It took those first Christians some time to realize God's timetable wasn't the same as theirs.

So when they realized maybe Jesus wasn't coming back as soon as they thought, some Christians named Matthew, Mark, Luke, and John decided to start putting the "good news" of Jesus into writing. Their versions of Jesus' life were taken as official because they were supposedly written by actual disciples, though we don't know that for sure. Besides, we all know that the Gospels don't always tell things in the same way or sequence. Mark has no birth or growing up stories about Jesus. Matthew and Luke do, but tell them differently. John tells the meaning of Jesus' life, so his Gospel is more theology than history. Paul's experience of the Risen Jesus was as a voice out of a blinding light, but he wrote about it before the Gospels were written.

Q: But don't those differences and contrary stores cast doubt on them, make them less credible?

A: That's one way to see it. But to me, those variations make the Gospels more believable, more credible, not less. The writers didn't collude to tell the same, seamless story with no rough edges. If that had been their intention, don't you suppose they'd have gotten together and polished up their stories, and their part in them, instead of so honestly leaving in discrepancies and disclosing their blundering, their denseness, their denials, and one goof after another? But they didn't flinch or make themselves look good. Because they didn't do that, because there are variations, even contradictions, in what the authors remembered, their stories are more credible. Does that cause you to dismiss them as fiction?

Q: Not really. Those things happen all the time in different newspapers and articles on the same events. It's also true of histories of different periods.

A: The thing is, if Jesus' resurrection hadn't been central to their stories and their experience, I doubt that the writers would have even written the Gospels or that there would have been a church at all. We also have to realize that the Gospels were not written by historians. Even if they had been, Emerson was on target when he said that there is no history, only biography. The Gospels were written by people of faith who told of the impact that Jesus' life and work and death and resurrection had on them. It is through that impact that we know Jesus because, try as scholars have, we can't get back to an objective "historical Jesus," or the unadorned facts of his life, any more than we can for any other person, past or present. Life is too complicated and multi-layered for that.

So the Gospel writers were not only writing about things that happened in Jesus' life and things he did and said, but more, they were really writing about those things in a way that conveyed how they experienced Jesus and what Jesus meant to his followers, to the early church. They wrote the essence of the story because it wasn't possible to write the whole of it. Think of how many pages it would have taken to record everything that was said and happened in just one day, let alone three years.

Q: But forty years is a long time for interpretations to get exaggerated. Isn't that a possibility here? Take the story of Pentecost and the roaring wind and tongues of fire and everyone within hearing distance hearing in their own language, which the story says included every language on earth. You don't think something like that actually happened, do you? Couldn't the resurrection be similar to that?

A: Let me respond in reverse order. Of course there can be exaggerations in stories, even those based in historical events. But I don't think linking the resurrection to Pentecost works that way. There could have been some hyperbole in the Pentecost story because it would have been to the advantage of the struggling little early church to tell the story with the emphasis the writer did. But what advantage would there have been to exaggerate or hatch the resurrection story that involved them in a mission that was dangerous to their lives? On the contrary, the story made them look like fools and subversives!

But think about the Pentecost story for a minute. You asked if I thought something like that "actually" happened. Yes, I do. Do I think it "literally" happened? No, I don't. What's the difference? Well, do I think a love letter telling my beloved that my heart is on fire for her, that her eyes are emeralds, her hair like silk, her teeth like pearls, her breath like jasmine—I'll stop before I go too far here—would be describing my literal experience of her, or would you believe it was? No. She'd look like a Picasso painting. But would I be conveying my actual, metaphorical experience of her, and would she understand that? Yes. That's really why so many fundamentalists miss things— because they want everything to be literal. And they don't realize that literalism is reductionism.

Q: So, if the guy was writing history, why didn't he tell it like it was on Pentecost? Why did he put it like an animated movie? What do you think really happened then?

A: I think what happened was what Luke wrote. The truths of something can be conveyed in poetic ways, symbolic ways. Are they fictions? Not exactly. Symbols point to a reality in which they are rooted, but that reality is somehow beyond literal description. Hook me up to a monitor while I am with my beloved, and you would get all kinds of data on brain activity, breathing rates, and skin electrical charges that are literal data, but they don't exhaust the *meaning* of my love.

Symbols are infused with larger meaning. Wedding rings are symbols of a complex relationship. Flags are symbols of entire nations. Bread and wine are symbols of the body and blood of Jesus. The wind and fire of the Pentecost story are symbols of an unseen Spirit, a Jesus-like Spirit, moving in among the disciples and visitors to Jerusalem. Just as music transcends the lyrics in a song, the fire and roaring wind conveyed the passionate vision and speaking of the disciples. The rhythm or beat of rap or hip-hop is contagious, even if the words are indecipherable to a lot of us. At a minimum, that's how people "got" Pentecost.

We don't necessarily think our way *to* truths we hold in our core. More often we think our way *from* them. We think our way from Pentecost, just as the crowd did on that first one. They listened to Peter preach about Jesus' life, crucifixion, and resurrection, and they began putting it all together as meaning something powerful, disturbing, appealing for them. They started thinking about life as being bigger than they'd thought it was and what they could do to live it differently.

That Spirit and those responses are what the church came from and continues in. Do I think Pentecost actually happened that way? Yes, in just that sense.

Q: But forty years is still a long time for lots of things to fog up about Jesus' life, isn't it?

A: Well, if you've got an oral tradition going, forty years isn't such a long time. Consider your memories of your grandparents, parents, uncles and aunts, friends, and the stories about them. Remember what your teachers taught fifteen, twenty, thirty years ago. These things are imprinted in our minds and bones. Don't you think that would be even more true of the Gospel writers, writing about what Jesus' life meant to them? Think back to what happened in 1964. What do you recall about that year?

Replies: "My daughter's birth." "Getting married." "Graduating from college." "The fallout from Kennedy's death." "Finding a job." "The Vietnam war." "The Civil Rights Movement."

A: Whoa, that's enough. Each of us remembers personal experiences as well as public events. Talking about those memories sharpens them for us. Take Dr. King's "I Have a Dream" speech in Washington that year. We've heard it replayed many times. If we tried to write about that speech and the Civil Rights Movement it gathered up so powerfully, we'd remember quite a bit of it—but not all of it, and not the same things. It wouldn't be literally, entirely accurate, but it'd be close to what Dr. King said and what happened then. Forty years isn't such a stumbling block to the truth we'd tell about it.

Historians who research the sources and study the archives might be more accurate about details and convey more information, but they would not necessarily be more truthful than we would. Historians are compelled to eliminate much of the anecdotal, relational stuff that happened, things that would flesh out an additional true, different, and yet important dimension of the more documented historical versions, such as with the Civil Rights Movement. People's stories carry a meaning that is more than the facts.

Q: Are you saying that we get hung up on specifics and miss the proportional value of things?

A: In a way, I guess I am. What often happens as a result of what's called "critical investigation" of historical events is that either it makes some people take the inevitable lack of the verifiability of some details as reason to dismiss the entire event—in this case, the Christian faith itself. Or it makes other people take those same unverifiable details and insist on them as proof that the entire event is literally correct and, again in this case, validates the Christian faith as unquestionably true. I think both responses miss the point and lose the true proportions of God and human beings.

The God of the Gospels doesn't need defending and can't be dismissed. Denied, doubted, labeled as superstitious, disagreed with, of course. Thought about, worshiped, trusted, lived out, certainly. But conclusively proved or disproved, no. Our response to God is a choice because we're free, not coerced. The choice makes a big difference for the chooser and the world. That choice is what faith is about. But it isn't necessarily a blind choice.

Q: I'd like to change the subject a little and ask what you think Jesus would say about the war in Iraq if he were on earth today.

A: That's changing the subject a lot! For starters, I'd guess Jesus probably wouldn't say much about the war directly. He didn't seem to say much about world events or big social issues of his time. He focused a whole lot on the kingdom of God, not much on the kingdoms of earth. He cared more about the decisions that people made about their lives and relationships than about how they might overthrow Rome, more about meeting people's needs than mobilizing political movements. He was more concerned about challenging leaders' hypocrisy than championing rebels' hyperbole, more with exercising spiritual authority than grasping for political power, often to the disappointment of his own disciples. He wasn't interested in being a king or recruiting armies. He just wasn't the kind of Messiah people expected, then or now, and that's probably why so many finally bailed out on him, then and now.

But Jesus did say things that could be taken as relevant to war and government: "Blessed are the peacemakers, for they will be called children of God." "Love your enemies and pray for those who persecute you." "If you forgive others their trespasses, your heavenly Father will also forgive you." "Do to others as you would have them do to you." "Why do you see the speck in your neighbor's eye, but do not see the log in your own eye?"[5] So I don't think he'd advocate or support a preemptive war or any kind of war, for that matter.

Then there was hard stuff in the woe passages in Matthew, such as, "Woe to you . . . For you tithe mint [and whatever, dill or cumin] and have neglected the weightier matters of the law: justice and mercy and faith. It is these you ought to have practiced without neglecting the others. You blind guides! You strain out a gnat but swallow a camel!"[6] And remember that when a disciple whipped out his sword and cut off the ear of one of those who came to arrest Jesus in Gethsemane, Jesus said, "Put your sword back into its place; for all who take the sword will perish by the sword."[7]

Jesus had a certain partiality for the poor, the sick, the socially excluded, and he told his followers that doing something for the least of these was doing it to him.[8] The key here is that Jesus applied this standard to the judgment of nations, not just individuals.

Q: But most people don't relate these statements to what a national government does.

A: It's questionable, if not faithless, for anyone to divvy up life into "God's part" and "our part," with our part being the most relevant to our lives and comfort. My guess is that Jesus would

5. *Sermon on the Mount, Matthew 5 ff*
6. *Matthew 23:23-24*
7. *Matthew 26:52*
8. *Matthew 25:31 ff*

say to us, "If you take to heart and do what I've taught you, and how I've lived, then you'll be able to figure out what your country should be and do."

If Christians like us tried consistently to do what Jesus did and said, it would have powerful consequences in political and social and national arenas. Dominic Crossan says Jesus' practice of eating with women, tax collectors, prostitutes, outcasts, as well as the rich and powerful, was a rebellion of inclusion that was contrary to the exclusion norms of the time. Jesus was not only saying but *showing* that a system that discriminates against people or dehumanizes them is wrong. Such a demonstration of breaking down religious and social barriers was one reason the power brokers came down on Jesus. What he did had political implications.

Q: But isn't it almost impossible to connect personal morality to political power? To get political power requires making deals, tip-toeing on the edge of deceit and corruption. And, almost by definition, doesn't personal morality get taken down in that process?

A: That's pretty cynical, isn't it? Besides, "almost impossible" doesn't make something impossible, just hard. Politics does involve compromises because no person or side is completely right. But compromises don't have to undermine integrity or involve deceit or corruption.

I think Jesus linked faith and personal morality to political affairs in one well-known instance. Remember when the religious leaders asked Jesus the hot-button question of whether or not it was lawful to pay taxes to the emperor? By "lawful," they meant according to their religious law. A "yes" answer would have gotten Jesus in trouble with the religious authorities, and a "no" answer would have gotten him in trouble with the Roman authorities.

You know what Jesus did: He told them to show him a coin, and he asked them whose image it was. They said, obviously, "The emperor's." Then Jesus made this seemingly ambiguous comment: "Give, therefore, to the emperor the things that are the emperor's, and to God the things that are God's."[9]

There it is! Give the emperor or government what you owe, namely taxes, service, even obedience up to a point. But Jesus was also subtly reminding them that the image on the coin was *not* the image of God, and that in itself was a radical thing to say in that society—or in any society, including our own. Christians and Jews believe human beings are made in the image of God, so we are to give God what we owe God, which is our very lives, our selves, our ultimate loyalty, our highest, deepest love. That's a powerful claim, and it has moral and political consequences.

Q: That's still quite vague. How do we know what Jesus meant, specifically or practically?

A: What he said doesn't resolve our dilemma, but it does tighten our discomfort. Isn't that probably the point of his statement: that emperor is not God, that country is not God, that our highest allegiance is not to our country or its government but to God. This is an important distinction and confronts us with a tough dilemma about which we have to freely make our specific choices. Jesus didn't spell out the details. That's left to us.

A critical contention between Rome and the Jews was that Rome believed Caesar was one of the gods and had the prerogatives of the gods. The Jews—Jesus being one of them—didn't believe that in the least. Disputes between variations of those views go on today in our confusion about whether our highest loyalty is to God or country. Trying to deal with it by fusing the two doesn't work! Jesus' radical distinction between the two dares us to weigh our country's policies and actions on the scale of our loyalty to a Christlike God and to respond accordingly.

For another thing, I don't think Jesus was saying that having a lot of coins with Caesar's image on them meant giving more allegiance to Rome or its counterpart, or letting it buy

---

9. *Matthew 22:15-22; Mark 12:13-17; Luke 20:20-26*

our silence or collusion on issues and policies that give some of us an advantage at the expense of aggravating, or of not alleviating, the burdens of the poor or the aged or children or the sick or oppressed in this, or any, country.

Q: Do you think Jesus was a pacifist?

A: He certainly spoke of peace a lot, blessed people with the word "peace." At yet, at one point he said, "I have not come to bring peace, but a sword."[10] Granted, that was in the context of people in families responding differently to him, but still, that's not doctrinaire pacifism, is it? I see Jesus as one who practiced aggressive nonviolence. I think he was a lot tougher and more confrontational than he's usually portrayed.

Over time, many Christians have determined that not all wars are equally wrong or bad. Many theologians have developed the theory of the "just war," where the "justness" of a war depends on several criteria: as the last resort, as a response only to an immanent threat, as being for a clearly just cause, as protecting civilian populations to the greatest extent possible, as being conducted by legitimate authority, and so on. I suppose World War II would qualify—at least until Hiroshima. But because of nuclear weapons, many today would insist there is no such thing as a "just war" now.

I think any war breaks the human heart, the heart of Christians, the heart of God, because love makes the heart vulnerable. Therefore reason pursues disarmament. In that way I think we're all pacifists, aren't we, even though we might reluctantly support a "just war" if persuaded it really is just, and not about vengeance or panicky fear about our security.

Q: Couldn't your answer about Jesus and the Iraq war and social issues be criticized as the position of liberal politics and not the Christian faith?

10. *Matthew 10:34*

A: It could be and it has been, by some. A few months after 9/11 and shortly after we went to war in Iraq, I spoke in a church in a heavily conservative Republican suburb of New York City. When I finished, one guy said, "You have just given us the same old liberal line." Some others agreed.

I said, "Maybe I have. But let me assure you that what I've said is, for me, rooted in my faith and my view of Jesus' life. I also assure you I love this country as much as you do, and what I've said is my 'lover's quarrel' with it. Isn't that at least as patriotic as unquestioning acquiescence to whatever my country does? So let me ask, as a Christian, 'What would you do to make this beloved country better?'"

Their first response was that they thought the country was pretty good the way it was. I said, "That isn't my question. My question is, as a Christian, what would you do to make it *better*?" I think that question was as close to divinely inspired as anything I've ever said because it enabled us to press beyond the liberal *versus* conservative political arguments. As *Christians*, we had a very long, lively discussion of the issues. A lot of people who would have sat on the sidelines in silence in a political argument were moved to put their views forward, and they were sometimes surprised by how the implications of what they were saying were at odds with their knee-jerk political allegiances. They discovered that the planks in Jesus' platform were really not the same as the planks in either the Democrat or Republican platforms. So they were left to think about choices differently than they had before.

Our faith may not legislate absolute answers, but it deepens us by framing life's question in a different way. That's what I think the church should be about these days.

Another example of this issue is when our congregation was criticized for becoming a Public Sanctuary Church in the mid-eighties, when we took a Guatemalan family into our church as political refugees, not illegal aliens. That wasn't a politically-driven decision but a decision made by the congregation after consideration of whether God or government was our highest loyalty.

When I went with the Congressional Delegation of Bob Edgar and Ted Weiss to Central America a few months later, we met with Christian-Base camps in El Salvador. These were peasants who were claiming their land, their rights, their freedom. We saw the same thing in Nicaragua where Roman Catholic priests were government leaders. The Roman Church was upset about these things and wondered what those people were doing. The peasants told the church, "What we are doing is studying the Bible together. We're trying to live like we're Christians." But to the church, that sounded like communism and it told them to stop. The peasants were anything but "godless communists." They were just challenging established authority of both church and government, and those institutions didn't like that.

The gospel isn't a political movement, nor does it advocate violence. But it is revolutionary, and it has political consequences. So it can be costly. Jesus showed that.

Q: I don't think of myself as having a relationship with Jesus. Over the years you have helped me understand the possibility of having a relationship with God, as in your prayer that begins, "Eternal God, lead me now out of the familiar setting of my doubts and fears . . ."[11] Maybe what I haven't understood about you is the way in which you see God through Jesus because, to me, you seemed to go straight to God. I'm beginning to think I misunderstood you. Did I?

A: If you did, the responsibility is partly mine for not being clear enough. My whole mustard-seed faith is in a Christlike God. But you're right. I did, and do, focus more on God than on Jesus Christ because that's what I believe Jesus did. He didn't pray to himself; he prayed to God. He didn't talk about himself; he talked about God and the kingdom. He didn't point to himself; he pointed to God. H. Richard Niebuhr talked about "Jesus-olatry," which he saw as replacing the sovereignty of

11. *Ted Loder, "Lead Me Out of My Doubts and Fears,"* Guerrillas of Grace.

God with the person of Jesus. I think it's easy to fall into Jesus-olatry, and I may have over-reacted against it. Yet the truth is, Jesus is central to my belief about God, without saying that he represents everything I believe about God. I believe Jesus shows us *enough* about what and who God is, but he doesn't reveal *everything* about God. I prefer to say "God is Christlike" because that's a more open and more mysterious way of referring to God.

Q: Don't you think the problem for most people, for me, is that we want more certainty than we can really have? So preachers of all kinds compete to sell that to us.

A: Possibly. Let me be brief here. We can't honestly get absolute certainty out of the Gospels. We can get assurance. We can probably get more certainty out of St. Paul, who is much more "off with their heads" than Jesus was. But history and experience have shown Paul wasn't right about everything either, and that in itself is a dollop of uncertainty in this soup. We have "Blessed Assurance," but not so much because "Jesus is mine," but because I/we are God's.

Q: Jesus means a lot to me, so I remember what you said after visiting Bill Coffin a few weeks ago, particularly about how important Jesus is to him. Could you talk about your conversations with him?

A: People don't understand Bill very well if they consider him to be only a religious spokesperson for liberal causes, or just define him as primarily a prophetic preacher. I've always known him first as preacher of the gospel. Before all else, he is a Christian who believes in Jesus Christ. What he preaches and stands for about peace and justice, civil rights and disarmament, and every other concern is rooted in the gospel and his faith in Christ. He's really an evangelist, a warrior for Christ. To use St. Paul's analogy, Bill puts on the whole armor of God, not just part of it.

Q: But you can see how people would put him squarely in the liberal camp, can't you?

A: Sure I can. It's *why* he's there that is dismissed or over-looked by people. As I see it, being liberal means being as concerned for justice as for freedom, as concerned for the poor and oppressed as for the wealthy and powerful, as concerned about alliances for peace and disarmament as about a strong defense and national security, as concerned about the environment as about economic growth, as concerned about racism and inadequate education as about fair taxation and irresponsible government spending. Being liberal involves an open attitude toward issues and people, not a closed one. Religiously, it means believing God is working toward a new heaven and a new earth among us even now, and our trying to discern and be part of that work.

Bill Coffin is a Christian who challenges power when he thinks it's wrongly exercised, no matter which party, president, church, or corporation is wielding it. James Carroll writes of being thrown in jail with Bill and some others for trespassing in the United States Capitol during an anti-war demonstration in 1972. There they sat in the dark of the jail in the middle of the night when Bill's voice rolled from his cell down the hall singing "Comfort Ye My People" from the *Messiah*. That scene reveals the essential Bill Coffin as deeply Christian and courageously faithful, yet one who is a Christian realist, to apply a Reinhold Niebuhr term. Bill is one of the great Protestant Christian prophetic voices of the twentieth century. Yet he also has worked with Jewish and Catholic leaders and people, as well as with agnostics and people of other religions, who respect and love him.

Q: I've never heard the term "Christian realist" before. What does that mean?

A: It means a lot more than I could explain. Christian realism involves rejecting biblical literalism, taking history seriously in all its complexity while seeing it as the arena of God's struggle with humans. It means granting that there is evil in the world that needs to be resisted, as well as psychopathic people who need to be contained, and acknowledging critical human limitations.

I suppose a condensed explanation is that Christians, particularly progressive Christians, need to deal with the world as it is, not as we wish it were, if we want to have any impact on it. It means being willing to get bloody and dirty, as Jesus did, in taking on the world in the service of God's kingdom; to deal with it realistically but not to be dishonest, or arrogant in the process. It means to make choices between imperfect options, to take stands in the gray areas and not wait for a black or white clarity that never comes. It means, as Niebuhr put it and I've said before, to be less concerned with the purity of our actions than with the integrity of our compromises, a caution long since branded into my mind. Only fools and tyrants think we can live in the world and act morally without compromises.

I'd also add that it means meeting complicated issues faithfully with our best ethical shot, then leaving the outcomes to God. It's sort of like my loaves and fishes and leftovers analogy. It means *enough* isn't *everything*, but something is better than nothing, and that there will always be leftovers to carry us into tomorrow.

Q: Why don't we hear more about this position? Surely it isn't limited to just Protestants. Aren't there a lot of Catholics and Jews who would agree with much of what you just said?

A: I think there are. The Catholic Berrigan brothers, Dorothy Day, and Rabbi Abraham Heschel are just a few examples. I think much of the reason we don't hear these different views is that most mainline Christians have been conditioned to be way overly concerned with the purity of our actions, to use Niebuhr's words again.

Since no one ever acts from a single motive or a pure one, we back off discussing critical issues in the mistaken notion we're being good Christians by doing that. If Jesus had done that, he would have died of old age rather than on a cross as a young man—which may be another reason we back off and remain disengaged. We fear for our jobs, our image, our standing among friends. We mistake congeniality for genuine community and so avoid controversial issues as if they were patches of poison ivy.

Too often we let our silence suggest agreement with what someone else says, without taking the little risk of saying, "Well, here's what I think, and why I think it is because I'm a Christian." For the most part, we don't do that very well. Morality gets reduced to avoiding expletives, obeying traffic laws, paying taxes, supporting the United Way, saluting the flag, making nice, and being liked.

Q: Many don't back off and do speak out about what we believe about issues, but it doesn't seem to make much difference in this social climate. Are you very optimistic that it ever will?

A: I'm more optimistic it'll make a difference if we *do* speak out than if we *don't.* We never know how a person's mind or heart gets changed, or what ripple effect speaking out might have. But you raise an excellent point about why we might back off from hard issues. We've also been conditioned to emphasize the morality of individual acts while de-emphasizing the morality of public policy. We evaluate candidates' religious character by what they say or do individually, or if they belong to a church or synagogue, rather than evaluating what they advocate or support and how that measures up with what we believe are just, peace-making, and compassionate policies that give evidence of taking Matthew 25 seriously.

We live in a time when Good Samaritans have to get organized. We need to get our views and reasons out there in the wider public arena. A couple of days ago I gave a copy of Bill Coffin's book *Credo* to a guy across the alley who is a political consultant for a non-incumbent candidate for the U.S. Senate. I told him the book was full of quotes and ideas the candidate could use. A few days later he yelled across the alley, "Hey, thanks for that book. It's good stuff. I didn't know anyone was saying that in churches."

Individuals like us need to find and support agencies and groups making such an effort. There is a Guatemalan saying that one twig alone can be broken; ten twigs together cannot be broken. It isn't just *my* faith that matters; it's *our* faith. If we don't get organized, the ultra-conservative voices are heard as *the* Christian position on whatever the issue may be, and the media reports it that way as if they're the only show in town.

Once Jan and I gave Fred Shuttlesworth a ride back to his hotel after he spoke at our church. Fred Shuttlesworth was one of the prime movers of the Civil Rights Movement, especially in Birmingham, Alabama. He was a real gutsy guy. His house was bombed, and he was threatened all the time. But the freedom song "Ain't Gonna Let Nobody Turn Me 'Round" fit him perfectly.

Fred said that after Dr. King was killed, the Civil Rights Movement sort of faded off the front pages. When Ralph Abernathy succeeded Dr. King, he complained about that to Fred. Finally, Fred said, "Ralph, when you *do* front page stuff, you'll *get* on the front page."

The point isn't for our alternative view of the Christian faith to get on the front page, but it is to let people know that there are other ways of being a Christian than just being a far-right fundamentalist. To do that takes organization. That's why it's important for us to support the National Council of Churches, for example, because they advocate things we believe are essential to the gospel. It's hard to balance between institutional responsibilities and personal beliefs about what the church should be and do. But integrity and faith necessitate managing that balance with integrity. I know we can deal with hard issues without either gutting the church of its relevance or destroying it as an institution. And I also believe we can't get to the real joy of the gospel without meeting its challenges.

Q: I'm going back now to Sherwood's death and what you said earlier about the resurrection. You talked about the relationships that Jesus had with people as being part of his resurrection, that there was something between them that had even more reality than any one of them had individually.

A: I think that is something of what Jesus meant when he said that the kingdom of God is among us, which is to say, it's between us. It's pretty amazing that Jesus came back to be among the very people who sold out on him. You and I would think that's the last group he'd come back to be with. We might think that they had their chance, and they blew it, so Jesus should have gone on to someone else, something else.

Q: It would be all over for most of us! Thank God, Jesus came back to the people he did.

A: Which means he came back to us—to our leaders and our enemies, to Sherwood and the Zapalla family, to everyone who is grieving and struggling. So we keep hoping and praying as we leave here and live our way into the world and the kingdom.

Years ago, in a small circle of people passing the bread and cup of communion to each other, the person next to me looked me in the eyes as he passed those elements and said, "Ted, here he comes again." Even so, the whole world is sacramental, beloved friends. In my heart I say your name and to each I say, keep your heart open, for place-by-place, moment-by-moment, "Here he comes again."

Fifth Sharing

Lord, we come together with each other and with you in a serious time, with serious concerns about serious matters. Enable us to take ourselves less seriously now, that we may learn to take you more seriously and be lightened by your Presence and your grace.

In your own time and for your own purposes, find us in our seeking, strengthen us in our sharing, abide with us in our restlessness, liberate us from fretfulness to serve your kingdom and care for each other and our neighbors. Enchant us into becoming like children, laughing, asking, imagining, and trusting you as the God and Father-Mother in whose spirit we live and move, have our being and pray. Amen.

It's good to see everyone and it's good to be together again. So, on with the questions.

Q: I'm feeling pretty negative about religion and churches in general. Why do so many people and churches promote things that hurt or demean people or treat them as if they're stupid? How can people buy into such rigid, oppressive, simplistic positions?

A: People are drawn to black-and-white, simplistic answers even if in their heads they might be humming that old song, "It ain't necessarily so." Maybe they're just too busy to think about complex issues, so they believe what the so-called "experts" tell them, since those experts claim to know God's mind. So guarantees of certainty trump truth, and pledges of security blur vision.

I read an article recently on the ethics of conviction. It said that, for increasing numbers of people, if you have strong enough convictions and act on them, you're doing the right thing. Ethically, sometimes religiously, that means strength of conviction overrides troubling questions and discomforting facts, and redefines truth to suit its views. That's what makes people fly airplanes into buildings in the name of Allah, or drop bombs on civilian populations in the service of God's kingdom. It also suggests why Jesus cautioned, ". . . you will know them by their fruits. Not everyone who says to me, 'Lord, Lord,' will enter the kingdom of heaven, but only the one who does the will of my Father in heaven."[1] The issue is less convictions than actions: how what we do matches up with our loyalty to the God we see in Jesus.

We are called to think as well as pray. As Bill Coffin says, "Christ came to take away our sins, not our minds." Reason is not the adversary of faith or religion. Neither reason nor religion is able to explain or to banish the ultimate mystery and truth of life and the world. It's arrogant and mistaken for either to try. We probably can't *think* our way *to* faith, but we surely can think our way *from* faith. Reason can help clear the way to faith, yet not quite get us there, because thinking can only clarify our choices; it is our heart that makes them.

Q: I have a question about that as a scientist. I've been amazed by the blueprint of reality so tightly held and marketed by ultraconservative people, no matter what. How do we maintain open sensitivity to them, consider facts that matter, and still keep passionate about our beliefs?

A: I do it by being willing to have everyone mad at me at some time or other about some issue or other, but not all at the same

1. Matthew 7:20-21

time. And it helps to realize that all of us can get dogmatic, not just the "other guys." One of the real pathologies of our time is that we get locked into our positions—some of them passionate and dogmatic—and then ugly arguments displace any dialogue. We become threatened, alienated, polarized, deaf to any truth in the others' views, and that rules out mutual learning and win-win negotiations.

The heart of Protestant Christianity is a commitment to the continuing reformation of the church. The Reformation didn't end in the sixteenth century; it just began then. It's going on today, hopefully. It's based on the reality that no person or institution controls God or speaks for God. Faith is dynamic, not static; a process, not a completed belief system; a process in which we are all necessary, equal, and valuable to each other.

Martin Luther, the point guy of the Reformation, put the matter this way: "We're saved by grace through faith." We're not redeemed by stacking up chips of right doctrines—or virtues, or prayers, or brilliant thoughts, or impressive resumes—in some sort of a poker game with God. Luther challenged church authority, and the reformation began. Once Luther pulled the cork, more bubbles came popping out in the form of other churches, interpretations, and emphases. The bubbles can't be put back in the bottle, thank God.

Q: Thank God? Are you saying that the ongoing Reformation is protection against the excesses or abuses of any church, ultraconservative or not? I'm not sure I follow that.

A: Theoretically, or theologically, that's what I'm saying. Practically, it doesn't always work that way, does it? Even so, the history of the Reformation has taught us a few lessons.

One is how easily, almost inevitably, reformers mutate into enforcers. They become as stubbornly dogmatic as the leaders and institutions they set out to reform. Unless the Reformation spirit prevails, the enforcers dominate. And though they try, no church, no religious group can really enforce their views. Tragedies happen when they try. Tragedies such as inquisitions, witch hunts, torture; tyrannies such as those of Osama bin Laden, Al Qaeda, the Taliban in Afghanistan. The terrorism of 9/11. The ruthlessness, at least in Arab eyes, of our "God bless America" retributive killing of tens of thousands of Iraqi civilians. The mercilessness of the Palestinian–Israelian tit-for-tat. The character/religion assassinations by right-wing Christian evangelists calling Islam an evil religion. The hard-line arguments against both birth control *and* abortion in an attempt to enforce a single, oppressive ideology on women and families.

God doesn't enforce. God indicates, invites, urges, constantly works to reform us. The gospel is about a dynamic process, and the Reformation confirms that. The church's mission is to keep thinking, keep finding new dimensions of good news, keep discerning what God is doing in our time because God didn't run out of ideas five hundred years ago, or fifty, or five, or yesterday.

Q: You said the Reformation taught us a couple of things. That's one. What's another?

A: Well, another thing the Reformation and its aftermath taught us is that there is not just one right way to think or worship or serve God. There are many ways. No one way can really claim to be the only way, or even the best way. If we admit no one can escape the limitations of time and knowledge and culture, we can stop that kind of power struggle and start learning from each other without making accusations against each other.

I'm reminded of the story of the pastor praying one morning when she hears a voice saying, "What do you want, my daughter?"

The pastor is startled but assumes the voice is God's. So she asks, "Lord, I pray for peace, but is there ever going to be an end to war?"

The voice replies, "Not in *your* lifetime, my daughter."

The pastor sighs and asks, "Then, Lord, I pray for the church. Will there ever be an end to the bickering and arguing and contention in the church?"

The voice replies, "Not in my lifetime, my daughter."

Of course, it's too pessimistic to think that in God's lifetime churches won't stop their power struggles and learn from each other, but you get the point. Faith compels us to keep stepping out on the call and the promise of a real round-table dialogue among all churches. Hope keeps us on the move after we step out.

Q: But what confuses me is how many different views of God there are, so many claims about who God is and what God wants, whose side God is on. How do we deal with that?

A: That's probably one of those questions we won't get an answer for in our lifetime. I think part of the confusion stems from power brokers and governments putting on the mantel of a religion to legitimize irreligious policies, going way back to the divine right of kings on down to our own time. There's more than a touch of that practice in most countries, even in our own. Presidents and citizens make "God Bless America" our second national anthem and a public appearance sign-off. It implies God is on our side and sanctions whatever we do and are. Elected officials claim to have God's endorsement for all kinds of public and private policies, in collusion with corporate or institutional powers with self-interest agendas. No wonder President Eisenhower warned us of the military-industrial complex.

It's time for evaluating and clarifying what we mean by referring to "God." Millions speak of God. Do we really know what they mean by that word? Do they? It's the season to ask and answer that question publicly. Probably Christians won't end up agreeing, but we may end up with some clarity about our differences and their implications for our life together as a nation and the issues we face in the human family.

Here's something I keep coming back to about God. H. Richard Niebuhr used to quote Luther's comment, "Whatever, then, thy heart clings to and relies upon, that is properly thy God." Niebuhr updated that by saying God is whatever you give your loyalty to and get your sense of worth from. That gives us a baseline in thinking about God.

To consider honestly what we're loyal to and what gives us our sense of worth helps us determine what kind of God we really trust—personally and as a people. To see and confess how we really operate in the world might startle us. To see what we're really most loyal to or get our biggest sense of worth from would probably mean we have several gods: our self, our country, our work or family or friends or bank accounts or church. The list would be long and change with our moods. The rub is that none of those little gods are necessarily bad, but none of them is sufficient for our lives and spirits. When we confuse any of those good little gods with God as Jesus talked about and demonstrated, we get snarled in a knot. It's not just how much faith we have or how passionately we believe, but what kind of a God we believe in. What kind of a God would support what we're saying and doing? That's the bottom-line issue.

If, as Christians, we say we believe in a Christlike God, then we mean we are loyal to that God and get our basic sense of worth from that God. We need to continually evaluate and respond to other good or bad things—self, family, work, country, enemies, sickness, death—according to how we grasp, or are grasped by, that Christlike God. The danger lies in the reverse: evaluating and responding to God by how we grasp, or are grasped by, these things.

Q: Do you really think doing any of that will change the church and the world?

A: I think it could if the church helped us figure out what it means to live that way and supported us in doing it. Then we'd have an edge to us. We'd take risks, contest society's values, be humble in the sense of being ready to be humiliated in walking with God.

Not only individuals but faith institutions need to speak out and take action. We need to join in supporting prophetic leaders and churches and organization, such as the National Council Churches. We need to be involved in advocacy groups that hold our political leaders and their followers, and us, accountable. It's not about political partisanship, it's about public morality from our Christian faith perspective. It's about taking our personal morality into the public arena. We need to press for our values relative to issues of poverty, medical care, women's rights, environment, global warming, funding public education. We may not prevail but that's not the point. Entering the fray and witnessing to what we believe about God is the point.

Words are cheap if they aren't rooted in deeds. We can say anything. What matters is what we do for justice and peace, love, and hope. It's not just volunteering in soup kitchens, which is excellent, but it's joining the struggle to eliminate poverty itself. It means our faith getting involved over its halos politically, economically, and socially. It means thinking and acting in and out of the religious box. That struggle will cost us, but we've got to get over wanting only changes that don't disturb our comfort level. That would make a big difference in the world—and who knows the ripple effect of that on the larger world?

Q: As I look at the world, it seems to me a lot of conflicts, violent and otherwise, are between different religions, like in Northern Ireland, the Middle East, Malaysia, Sudan, other parts of Africa. Why should the church get involved in these conflicts?

A: When our congregation was in the process of becoming a Reconciling Congregation, people would ask me why we had to go public with our support of homosexual persons. I said because those who discriminate against gays and lesbians do so publicly, we need to make a public response.

That's also the reason we need to raise our voices and be heard on the issues that dehumanize, brutalize, and oppress people in the name of Christianity or any other religion. At the same time, we need to heed the warning to pick our enemies carefully because we're going to end up just like them. Even churches can become demonic in battling those considered to be demonic enemies. That often happens, and we need the larger faith community to restrain such responses. God help the church to be such a community.

We in the church also need to try to see the face of those we call enemies and not just make tooth-and-claw reactions to them. I know, for example, that my/our first and lowest impulse is to go tooth and nail after groups that sponsor suicide bombers. We need wise, honest, merciful, moral people in the communities of both faith and humanity to help us think and believe past that impulse. We need people to help us understand how those enemy groups see us because of the way we disrespect their culture or religion, or degrade them by exploiting their country's resources for our own use. We ourselves need to become those wise, faithful people. To say that is not blaming America but attempting to enlarge its vision. It is to suggest that we deal not only with symptoms but with underlying causes. Such understanding is essential to loving our enemies as Jesus told us to do.

Q: Does it matter? Will stating our view make any difference to people who only react emotionally?

A: Standing for what we believe matters enormously more than shutting our mouths and eyes. It matters to those whom we tell we are Christians. It matters for us to frame the questions and issues differently and to engage the world around us. And it *does* make a difference, if not in the short run, then in the long run.

Here's the critical piece: To love our enemies doesn't mean to be afraid to make them; but once made, we aren't excused from working at what loving them means in our time and circumstances without getting arrogant, angry, or disheartened. We can't do that without supporting and holding each other accountable. Then at the end of the day, we need to pray, "God bless and have mercy on us all."

Q: Can anyone actually all do that? It seems impossible. I'd flop before I got started.

A: You're right, it's not easy. Maybe it's impossible. But our charge is not to finish the job, just to keep working at it.

Sometimes I wonder about the people who gave the loaves and fishes to Jesus that day when he taught the multitude. Even if they thought it was a crazy idea, they probably figured, "Let's just do this and see what happens." Maybe Jesus himself was thinking that, even as he blessed the five loaves and two fishes and broke them and started passing pieces around.

Isn't that kind of risk what Christian freedom is about? Our freedom is not self-generated; it issues from trusting that there is another, far greater, wiser, more gracious power than any of ours at work in this world. Nothing is finally all up to us.

Even on what seem like Good Friday days, it's still an Easter world, no matter what. All is never lost. Even death—yours, mine, or anyone's—is not going to defeat God. The kingdom is coming, even as we pray all our lives and with our last breath for it to come. That's very hard to hang on to. We can do it only by hanging on to each other. That hanging on is the heart of the church at its best.

Q: No matter what the conflict might be, I feel there is no justification for exchanging a child's life for freedom or power or economic advantage. Where do the lines get drawn on that sort of thing?

A: Your question is close to the heart of every moral choice.

Toni Morrison's novel *Beloved* is about a slave mother who killed her baby girl to keep her from slavery and then lived with the disturbing, invisible presence of someone she called "Beloved," who was clearly the daughter she'd killed.

There's a story that came out of the Nazi holocaust of several Jewish families hiding in a location where Nazi soldiers were searching for them. One of their babies started crying. They smothered the baby to save their families.

Those actions may be extreme cases, but who can judge them as absolutely immoral? There's a hint of God's suffering, resurrecting presence in them, I believe. Our moral choices are rarely obvious and often can have a down side. That's why a morality of absolutes is fine in the abstract but not in the muck and mire of the multilayered world we live in. That's why anguish, not arrogance, is often part of making moral choices. That's why humility should mark most of our choices, not defensiveness or self-justifying excuses.

At the start of the Korean War in 1950, I was in college. I went to talk to a beloved older minister named Seth about why he'd been a Conscientious Objector in World War II. We sat on wooden boxes in his vegetable garden as we talked. I remember the smell of the tomato vines. He was a basketball fan, so at first we talked about my university team.

When I asked about him being a C.O., he reached over, picked a big, ripe tomato, and began to talk. "I became a C.O. after much thought and prayer because I decided that was what I should do as a Christian. It had a cost. I spent time in jail, then as an orderly living in a mental hospital."

He rubbed the tomato a minute and then said, "And yet, I also felt some guilt about being a C.O. because I was making a judgment on the situation I'd been part of that brought about the war. By being a C.O., I was dissociating myself from that situation and the people who'd shared it with me. I'm not sure I had a right to do that. I often think of the kids who fought and died in that war." He handed me the tomato and said, "Here, take this with you."

I'm not sure what he meant me to take, but the tomato is long gone and his story is in my bones. I think it describes our moral dilemmas and choices accurately and powerfully. It seems appropriate to your question. What do you think?

Q: I think I'd still be a C.O., but a less angry, self-righteous one. What about you?

A: I decided not to be a C.O. But I felt the anguish of that decision. To go off to war as a crusade against evil is simplistic and morally questionable, in my view. To do that is to create a climate in which looking critically at ourselves is labeled unpatriotic and irreligious, if not traitorous, a climate that gives us permission to do all kinds of things that are essentially contrary to what we say we believe as a people.

On the other hand, to do nothing after a surprise attack such as Pearl Harbor that kills thousands is not a defensible moral option either. Now, we're rightly horrified by terrorism and suicide bombers who target children, as Palestinians and Chechens have done. But are we right to reciprocate with actions that put enemy children in harm's way? On 9/11, among the three thousand American people killed was the twenty-five-year-old daughter of a Catholic friend of mine. He and his wife are not vengeful, just brokenhearted, a morally critical distinction.

Three thousand individual American deaths is tragic. So are the deaths of thousands of Iraqi civilians, including children, killed in war. Collateral damage may be inevitable, but it's not irrelevant. Iraqi families are as brokenhearted as American families were and are. Some might accuse me of being unpatriotic for saying that, but we need to be concerned that, in trying to overcome terrorists, we don't lose our humanity. As a Christian, I don't think God leads parades to or after a war. Nor should a nation use military service or support of war as a test of patriotism.

At the same time, I think there can be some situations that call for surgical military action. In that view, the biblical view of the world as a fallen place seems compelling. Sometimes military action is morally justified but never in a triumphalist way. I believe we should be extremely reticent to go to war except for the most urgent reason.

Q: So exactly what do you think Christians' response to war should be?

A: Contrition, compassion for all sides, courage not to demon-ize the enemy, wisdom in its execution, care for the young people who fight, and persistence in working for justice that eliminates the causes of war.

Perhaps the best statement of a faith orientation is Lincoln's Second Inaugural address near the end of the Civil War: "Both [sides] . . . pray to the same God, and each invokes His aid against the other. . . . The prayers of both could not be answered. That of neither has been answered fully. The Almighty has His own purposes. . . . With malice toward none, with charity for all, with firmness in the right as God gives us to see the right, let us strive on to finish the work we are in . . . to do all which may achieve and cherish a just and a lasting peace among ourselves and with all nations." Those words are profoundly consistent with Scripture, with trust in God beyond our own convictions, and deeply relevant to our time.

For us, a just and lasting peace depends on the conditions we create for future generations, for kids everywhere. It depends on not spending enormous sums on the military and making the building and supervising of prisons a growth industry, while squeezing our wallets when it comes to education, building schools, paying teachers, providing child care, after-school pro-grams—for starters. A just and lasting peace means taking seri-ously Jesus' saying that if anyone causes kids to stumble, they'd be better off if they were thrown into the sea.[2]

Q: So you're not a pacifist and don't think every Christian should be one?

A: War can sometimes be the best of awful choices, but the wounds it leaves mean that war is not a very good sign that we're doing the will of God or being faithful to God. I don't want to be too simplistic and say that every instance of war or killing is being unfaithful. But I would say that it is highly probable that being peacemakers is a far more faithful response to God.

2. *Mark 9:42; Luke 17:2*

I also need to add that I'm ideologically against war, and yet I can't honestly say I'd be against a particular war if I considered it to be just. I am committed to nonviolent resistance to injustice whenever possible, as in the Civil Rights Movement. But I am not a pacifist. Pacifists are our consciences but maybe not our minds. I am grateful for pacifists, yet I don't think it's a requirement for being a Christian. However, I certainly don't think a Christian can ever be a warmonger.

Q: You said that there are instances in which war could be justified. What would be such a case?

A: Probably the Civil War was justified. I think World War II was also such a case. Probably if the circumstances after World War I had been handled differently, World War II might have been avoided. But once 1938 came, resisting Nazi tyranny was justified. Nuclear weapons raises the bar for any war qualifying as just instead of being just unimaginable and unacceptable.

International military action of some sort might be justified, for example, to stop the genocide in Dafur in the Sudan. If you saw the powerful movie *Hotel Rwanda* or recall the stories of the terrible genocide there in the 1990s, you would probably think, as I do, that international military intervention would have been more justified than what we did by turning our backs on that horror. And political and economic interventions are often needed options to nip a war. Can we help the desert bloom like a rose for both Palestinians and Jews? Let's hope!

In any case, I believe Christians should press for more of our resources being used to alleviate conditions that lead to war rather than squandering them in endless development of ever more efficient weapons to wage war. I believe that would not only make the world more secure but would be more consistent with the kingdom of God than other options.

In this nuclear age, it's time to reconsider what our real interests are as Christians, as Americans, and as a human family irrevocably tied together in one destiny. To say with the prophet, "Let justice roll down like waters,"[3] doesn't mean we have to have detailed irrigation systems ready, but we do need to have some serious proposals for pumps and pipes under consideration. Otherwise, we're just talkers who will be dismissed as dreamers. But it won't hurt at all to work on getting more people to sign on to the vision of justice rolling down like waters.

Q: I bet none of that will ever happen.

A: Maybe not. But almost certainly it won't happen if we don't start thinking about our kids and grandkids and great grandkids, praying and planning, working and sacrificing toward the promise of the peaceable kingdom when the wolf shall live with the lamb, the leopard shall lie down with the kid and the calf and the lion and the fatling together, and a little child shall lead them. That's the vision of prophets. That, as well as nations not lifting up their swords—or missiles—against other nations and not learning war any more; people not hurting or destroying in all God's holy mountain; people pounding their swords—and missiles—into plowshares and silos for grain; people loving their enemies, and all that stuff.[4] That's the direction our Christian pilgrimage is headed, and I believe a Christlike God walks with us.

Q: That raises the question of where we should be spending our time. Should we be spending our time on a relationship with God or on a political agenda that conforms to our reading of the gospel?

A: I think it's a both/and, not an either/or. What are the two great commandments according to Jesus? Love the Lord your God with all your heart, mind, soul, and strength, and love your neighbor as yourself.[5]

3. *Amos 5:24*
4. *Isaiah 11:4 ff; Isaiah 2:4; Luke 6:27 ff*
5. *Matthew 22:37-40; Mark 12:29-31; Luke 10:25-28*

Q: But doesn't Jesus say the first commandment is the greatest?

A: Yes, but he linked them. I believe if we try to keep the first about loving God, we will move quickly to the second about loving neighbor. If we keep the second long and hard enough, it teaches us about ourselves, warts and all, and about God's love, and therefore what it means to love neighbors as ourselves. That brings us to our knees to love God and to seek strength to love others.

Occasionally someone claims that God speaks directly to them in an unmistakable way or through a mystical experience, and I don't question their experience. But for most of us, God speaks indirectly through other people. If I pay attention to other people, if I look in their eyes, if I really engage them, I encounter a mystery and a claim, which is that these human beings are really my brothers and sisters. These are persons in whom there is something sacred. These are persons I am called to love.

Q: Really? Some days people seem to be just slobs, barbarians, idiots. Where do we find these people you're talking about?

A: I know what you mean. But I recently read Marilynne Robinson's novel *Gilead* about an old preacher who was dying. At one point he said now that he was about to put on imperishability, just mere existence was the most amazing thing he could imagine. Just watching people laugh was an incredible sight.

I've had that sense, haven't you? There's a line about human beings in a poem by Czeslaw Milosz that goes like this: "They are so persistent, that give them a few stones and edible roots, and they will make a world."[6] That assessment may be a bit of an overreach, but still, it echoes the Genesis creation story when, after the sixth day, humans were put in the picture, God saw everything he'd made and said it was very good—roots, stones, and all.

6. *Czeslaw Milosz, "Throughout Our Lands: 9," New and Collected Poems, 1931-2001*

If you get past exterior images, you'll find the people I'm talking about in this room, on the street, in stores, restaurants, bars, planes, driving trucks, fixing roofs and toilets, everywhere—even in church. I have found them in the marches with Dr. King, in South Africa queuing up at 5 A.M. to vote, living on garbage dumps in Haiti, walking with the Mother's of the Disappeared in Guatemala. They aren't necessarily the most educated or attractive or successful people, but there's something about the stark reality of every human being that links us with each other, and to the Father-Mother of us all.

For me, the love of neighbor is where the love of God comes down and becomes incarnate, so to speak. I believe that's what St. John was saying in his letter when he wrote, "Those who say, 'I love God,' and hate their brothers or sisters, are liars; for those who do not love a brother or sister whom they have seen, cannot love God whom they have not seen."[7]

That's where I think the religious right people often get off the track. They don't talk much about justice for brothers and sisters who are poor, hungry, or sick. They feed them in soup kitchens and try to convert them, but they don't address the conditions that generate poverty, hunger, and illness. That's only half of morality.

Q: I come from a family that's very conservative. Living so far away, it's easy for me to rail against all their certainties about God and everything else. But when I go home to visit, here are these people who love me, and I love them. I don't know how to handle my frustration with their dogmatic belief system. I don't know how to separate my disagreement from my love of these people who believe they're doing what God wants. What do you say to that?

A: I know. In my first church it was always the biggest pain-in-the-necks who brought chicken soup when anyone in my family was sick. Muddies up the water, doesn't it?

7. *1 John 4:20*

One way to get at the problem is to honestly ask ourselves what is really in our self-interest. That's not a wrong or unChristian question. Taken as a faith question, it pushes us past either the hypocrisy of the shallow religiosity Jesus criticized or the cultural impulses of short-term responses. For example, I learned early on that it really isn't in my self-interest to avoid discussing issues with others who might disagree in order to be congenial, and then simmer and act out in destructive ways for myself and others.

I am still learning that my truest self interest isn't really in trying to prove the disagreeing and often disagreeable others wrong—though I confess I often succumb to that temptation and need to be honest about that. My deepest self-interest is to openly make my beliefs and positions as a Christian clear, let the chips fall, and hope the others may see something in what I say that may change something in and for them and, maybe, let something in their positions open me to new truths. My self-interest is to try to love them, listen to them, take them seriously, and be honest with them. My core self-interest is to grow in and through loving my neighbor honestly and humbly, and trusting God to work in the process.

Q: That raises the issue of reconciliation. It's hard to get past needs and biases and into the views and needs of others. I know reconciliation doesn't mean winning, but what does it actually mean?

A: I think there are three essential steps in reconciliation. Maybe more, but certainly these three: First, reconciliation involves honestly facing into the differences and what constitutes the breach between parties. Second, it involves the recognition and admission of our limitations, distortions, and responsibilities in causing the breach—hopefully by both sides. Third, it involves the need, the longing, on at least one party's part, to be reconciled to the other. Someone needs to risk taking the initiative, which pride makes it hard for us to do.

I think that having the courage and trust to take that third step depends on knowing the difference between being *connected* and being *engaged*. We're all connected because that's the way God made us and the world. That's the way things are, like it or not. We're slowly learning that what happens in Iraq affects the world. What happens in China affects the world. What happens to the poor in our country affects the whole country. Poverty anywhere in the world affects the whole world. Nuclear war between two nations affects all nations. AIDS, terrorism, epidemics, and global warming affect everyone. So does peace. Connection is a given.

But engagement is a *choice*. Can we push past the barriers of prejudice, certainties, greed, pride, gender, politics, nationalism, whatever, to really engage each other as human beings? Can we engage, be openly and honestly involved with each other in facing and working on the breach between us? Can the powerful take the initiative to engage the weak; the injurer, the injured; the well-off, the poor; the seniors, the young; Christians and Jews, Muslims—as well as the other way around in all cases? Those are questions I believe God asks us all the time.

I think Jesus models our answers. Reconciliation is precious but costly. It's a gift but takes work. It doesn't entail conformity or uniformity. The way to reconciliation is a constant effort in every dimension of our existence to engage in living deeply into the essential meaning of our being connected because God made the world that way and life depends on it. That's what I think reconciliation means and what Christians need to be about.

Q: My dilemma is this: Every day I make decisions on the run. People say, "Be the change you wish to see in the world" or "Follow your bliss," or "Keep the Ten Commandments, or "Ask 'What would Jesus do?'" In the midst of the helter-skelter of life, how do you make right decisions?

A: Tough question. This morning I read the paper about Smarty Jones not winning the Preakness horse race and losing the Triple Crown when it seemed everyone was pulling for him to win it. After the race, Smarty's jockey, Stewart Elliot, was asked why he rode Smarty the way he did. He answered, "In a horse race a jockey makes decisions in a split second. If you win they cheer, but if you lose, they blame and say, 'You shouldn't have done that.' Are they right? Who knows? Obviously, I didn't think so at the time." Most decisions we make are like that, and lots of people second-guess them and criticize us, maybe rightly.

Q: Hindsight is 20/20, right?

A: At best. The point is, we make decisions out of who we are, our experience and faith. Each of us is a person in process, not a finished product. The process involves a lot of things: our environment, family, education, our wrestling with our spirit, praying, thinking, listening, reading the Bible, watching other people. All of that shapes who we are and the decisions we make every moment. At times we have longer than a moment to make a decision, but often we don't. Plus, it isn't as simple as winning or losing.

The freedom of faith is not that we will always make the "right" decision. Like the jockey, we make the best decision we can make at the time and go on to make other decisions that might be different because of the experience gained in making a wrong one. In any case, we trust God to make something good out of any decisions we make.

We're free to be faithful, but we're also free *not* to have to be right. Faith and humility help us realize that it's okay to be just partly right or often not right because from that we learn about God and ourselves as "mere" but valued, valuable, valuing human beings. The freedom of faith is less about having to be right than being able to honestly say, "God have mercy on me, and on us all." With that, we join the fray with a different spirit.

Q: You've referred several times to our longing and said it's involved in being reconciled. I used to think being reconciled to something or someone meant being resigned to it, or them. Now I don't think it means that. I'm aware of St. Paul's statement that God reconciled us to himself in Christ, and yet I'm not sure what that means for me, personally. Can you talk a bit about all that?

A: You guys don't ask easy questions, do you?

Q: Are there any?

A: Not really. Anyway, the rest of that bit from St. Paul is that, after reconciling us to himself in Christ, God gives us the ministry of reconciliation.[8] The two parts go together: To accept God's reconciliation means accepting the ministry of reconciliation in our lives and our world.

Any sense of being reconciled to God without being reconciled, or working on reconciliation, with each other is spiritually and morally empty. We discover what it means to be reconciled to God when we take on the work of being reconciled with our brothers and sisters, however difficult they might be. I'm not saying the two actions are the same, only that they're inseparably connected.

Q: Is that where longing comes in? Are you saying love and longing are the same thing?

A: No, I'm not saying that. I'm trying to say that reconciliation with God involves a new way of seeing ourselves and other people. Simone Weill said that perfect attention is prayer. Paying attention gets us to our longing. We long to overcome whatever separates and alienates us from others or God. Some of it comes from attending to our guilt and fears, or to our deep loneliness,

8. *2 Corinthians 5:17-19*

or our constant sense of incompleteness. Some of it comes from our soul's stretching in the womb of time and hope.

All that is more a part of our longing, I think. We long for something that we're missing. We long for the healing of broken relationships and broken promises, the rebirth of wonder, the calming of restlessness, the now of eternity, the joy of lived connections. I believe longing is one of the ways God moves in us to signal the presence of the kingdom in our midst. Longing is not the same as desire. Desire is longing attracted to achievable but transitory ends or objects. Longing has a cosmic dimension that accompanies our sense of the sheer radiance of life, such as when we look at the stars or into a baby's eyes, or become aware of the presence of a sacred "Thou" in other people.

If we truly listen to our longing, we're nudged toward the work of reconciliation. We start approaching every person as an opening to God's kingdom in our midst. Embracing other people of all kinds, classes, genders, nationalities, races, orientations makes us, and them, more human. That's what I think longing and the ministry of reconciliation is about.

Q: Okay, but when I take a step toward reconciliation with someone I'm estranged from, it makes me feel very vulnerable. It's humbling to be dangling on that other person's response. How do I deal with the urge to just push the person away when God's kingdom seems kind of abstract?

A: You're right about the process being humbling. Plus, it's often hardest to reconcile with family members or those closest to us. But my experience is that humility is a basic factor of faith not in a phony, obsequious way but in being willing to be humiliated, to acknowledge our own mortality. By mortality, I don't mean just that we're limited in time, but that we're limited in knowledge, capacities, and experience as well. It helps us to realize and be grateful that we're being upheld in existence by all kinds of people, including those we're estranged from and need to be reconciled with.

Q: But what if I'm trying to mend a relationship and the other person or persons don't respond and stay hostile? What then?

A: Then you're learning humility and something of what's involved in being a human being trying to be faithful to God's kingdom, which is abstract only when we prefer it to be. Hard as it is, to work on reconciliation is to become more aware of the kingdom, which is reason enough to do the work. Of course, there aren't many guarantees, and there are a lot of bruises and oops in it, but many hurrahs as well. We're connected. Reconciliation is about living that out.

We all made our debut on this earth long after it started whirling around the sun, and long after human beings started tromping around on it. We didn't have anything to do with our getting here, as far as we know. So awareness of that carries a degree of humility and proportionality. Each of us is of great worth yet of little moment in this enormous universe, and it's hard to acknowledge that. But avoiding it is disastrous every which way. So in faith we ride that yo-yo. We take risks because in humility we have to, and because in love we long to. And the truth is, we're all vulnerable, though not everyone knows it and not many like it.

C. S. Lewis said in his book *Four Loves* that to love anything at all is to risk having your heart broken. The only way to avoid it is to not risk loving, to put your heart under lock and key where it won't get broken. But it will become unbreakable. I guess that's the real choice we have.

But reconciliation is more that just a personal or individual matter. In a real sense it's a corporate act. We borrow courage and support from each other in becoming reconcilers. We borrow knowledge and experience. That's what parenting and families are about. And neighborhoods and friendships. That's what joining with others to reconcile groups, races, genders, classes, and nations is about. That is what the church is about at its best. To risk being reconcilers makes us vulnerable, but it doesn't have to make us solitary.

Q: Loving is something that we Christians should be able to manage, but in reality, we seem to be like people in "The Sopranos." If somebody really messes us up, we want to whack 'em. We don't do that directly, but doing it vicariously or indirectly can be very satisfying, can't it?

A: Most of us know what you're talking about, both as figurative whackers and whackees, so yes, it can be satisfying. It's the dark side of our nature, isn't it? It's also part of the reason why so many people favor war: to whack people we don't like or who threaten us.

But I think it may also have something to do with our society, which is mostly based on competition at almost every level and so is mostly about power, winning, and "survival of the fittest" or the successful. That's what we're taught from cradle to grave. Yet we frequently learn that competition, which gives us something of a whacking license, also has a destructive down side. The *ends* of success and power do not justify whatever *means* it takes to get them, temporarily satisfying or effective as they may seem. So there's always a need and place, in and around us, for fairness and fidelity, and thus for compassion.

Q: It might be simple-minded to say it, but the deal seems to be if you kill enemies, literally or figuratively, you really don't need to worry about them any more.

A: It isn't that easy, is it? We still need to worry about those who are killed and those who killed them. Look at the aftermath of the Vietnam War over thirty years later. Rationalizing it all by saying that the enemy is evil doesn't make them so. Supposedly that makes killing them bearable. But does it? Really?

Anybody that I have ever known who has been in a war has continued to struggle with what they were a part of. When you kill, it's *human beings* you're killing, even though the cause might be just. It has a profound impact. Studies show that a large percentage of soldiers on the front lines of the World

Wars, on both sides, shot their guns in the air rather than at the enemy. Apparently, there is some aversion to killing each other that's hardwired into most of us.

Recent studies have discovered that human beings have so much trouble killing people that they have to be trained to do it. That is what the military does. The more technology enables soldiers to see the enemy just as targets on screens, not "like us," the easier it is to kill them. But even then, the first time a person kills another person, it is traumatic, and he/she never gets over it. Part of what happens in any war is that it inflicts not just visible wounds and casualties on both sides but also profound emotional and spiritual scars on those who do the killing. Killing is a violation of God's image we're all made in. And somehow we know it.

Q: Earlier you said reconciliation is not easy, and it doesn't come naturally. Why is it that so many of the things that matter, and that God seems to want us to be, don't seem to come naturally?

A: It's a dilemma, isn't it? Maybe part of it is the use of the word "natural." Maybe we should use the word "inclination." We could say we have the natural *capacity* but not the natural *inclination* to be or do what God wants us to. Our natural inclination is self-concern or self-advancement. But at our core, we also have the natural capacity for compassion, justice, peace, sacrifice, and love. It's just harder to tap into those, to claim those things about ourselves. We need help to do that, whereas we can claim and follow our contrary inclinations on our own, or with an assist from our society. Our freedom bears on the struggle between capacity and inclination.

Q: That helps, but go further with it, will you?

A: Well, I think our common experience is that we are a mix of elements, to use Shakespeare's word. We're trying to be integrated and live with integrity. We're also trying to get ahead and do what that requires. Mostly, we don't totally make it either way, though with the lure of social and economic rewards, we tend to be more inclined toward getting ahead than integrity.

And yet the truth of it is that we are at war within ourselves. One of the most powerful things St. Paul ever wrote was about our not doing the good that we want, but doing the evil we don't want. Inwardly, we may delight in God's covenant, but in our outward lives, we conform to another law that's at war with our inner self. That war makes us miserable. So we ask, "Who will rescue [us] from this body of death?"[9]

We experience that inner war, don't we? I certainly do. Counselors and therapists use psychological terms to describe the same experience. So do people with addictions. We all know what self-destructive behavior is because we're inclined toward it and are pretty good at it. We seem to lose our way in a maze of dollar signs, ME-ism, social seductions, and status games. We're inclined to believe the hype that we're suckers or dreamers if we don't put "number one" first, don't kiss up to climb up, don't be phony and do what's necessary to win since that's what's valued in our culture and economy. But all that triggers the inner war St. Paul's talking about.

The great theologian Thomas Aquinas put it something like this: It's the heart of sin that we use what we ought to enjoy, and enjoy what we ought to use. At least one thing this means is that we use ourselves and other people, and God, when we should enjoy them; and we enjoy things we should just use, and in doing that, misuse and abuse them and ourselves. That's another way to describe our inner war as well as our outer world.

Q: I'm pretty sure we all experience that war to some extent or other. But why can't we stop it, get out of it? Why does it keep plaguing us, even when we want to change things?

9. *Romans 7:14-25*

A: You're right, most of us do long to change, to be delivered from that body of death, as St. Paul calls it. We don't want to be addicts to something or some things anymore. We don't want to self-destruct, or hurt our families or other people, or rattle around in a busy but empty life. While there is a God-given spirit in us that nudges us in a different direction than the one society and our Eden-inclination seduces us to take, it is hard to actually move in that different direction. If it were quick and easy, which we all wish it were, maybe the self-help books that crowd the bookstores would be the answer. We need more than self-help, but pride gets in the way of our asking for it.

"Who will deliver me from this body of death?" St. Paul asks for us. Then he answers, "Thanks be to God through Jesus Christ our Lord." And there we are, back to our earlier discussion about salvation, how Jesus saves and the different ways God works in our lives and answers our prayers. Sometimes God works directly, but most times indirectly through all sorts of other people. But be aware that our natural inclinations will always collide with our natural capacity. So we never arrive at the end of the "different way" that faith represents. We get saved a dozen times a day, maybe more. Salvation is a process, and it takes the courage of faith and the persistence of hope to keep engaging in that process.

Q: My question is, no matter how hard you work at it, is reconciliation always possible? I haven't found it to be. What am I supposed to do then?

A: Surely in God's lifetime, reconciliation is always possible, but maybe not in ours—at least not if it involves betraying other critical faith issues like faith, justice, and peace. But only very reluctantly should we give up efforts to be reconciled.

It may be that the church is going to have to divide if an issue becomes irreconcilable, and we can't live with our disagreement. Obviously, the church has done that in the past. At the moment, gay rights have become a wedge issue in church and society. For some, that may make us shift from seeking reconciliation to seeking justice.

Remember, in his Gospel, John reported that when the religious leaders were arguing about what to do with Jesus, one of them said, "You do not understand that it is better for you to have one man die for the people than to have the whole nation destroyed."[10] That offers a terribly misguided religious sanction to a "Better him than us" attitude. No one can volunteer another person to abuse or death, or dehumanize another person just to save his or her own skin—or views. Not with spiritual justification, anyway. But often that's the attitude behind discriminating against other people or minorities. What kind of God would support our doing that? Not the one I see in Jesus Christ.

If some groups favor discrimination against blacks or Asians or Hispanics or homosexuals, then justice trumps reconciliation with such groups. If some people or politicians suggest, however subtly, that being poor or unemployed or underemployed is the fault of those in such situations, and no one else has any responsibility for them or the conditions that produce them, then justice trumps reconciliation with those people. If groups argue that being Arab or Iraqi or Iranian or North Korean, or whatever, makes a person less than human, then justice trumps reconciliation with those groups.

To trust God is not to wait until the train is leaving the station in the wrong direction. It's to begin laying the track for the train to go in a different direction.

Q: Do you think and feel the same way about the Pro-Life/ Pro-Choice conflict?

A: That's a very dicey subject. Both sides have moral positions, and it would be an enormous step forward if each side would concede that about the other and start an open dialogue.

The Pro-Life camp's insistence that human life is precious and should be protected is a moral position regarding

10. *John 11:50*

the sanctity of life. But their insistence that this position is absolute and without qualifications, no matter what the circumstances of a woman's pregnancy—or that the emergency use of "morning after" pills should not be prescribed in cases of rape, or that birth control should be illegal—severely compromises the morality of their position, especially when it leads to such tactics as bombing abortion clinics, killing doctors, and intimidating women.

The Pro-Choice camp's insistence that women's lives should be respected and that women have the right to choose a medically safe abortion is also a moral position. It affirms that women are highly valuable and competent to make moral decisions for themselves, in consultation with their God, doctor, mental health and spiritual advisors, according to the personal circumstances of their pregnancy. The Pro-Choice position protects the right of women to make that decision and not be restricted to women who can afford to go someplace where it's legal and safe. But the Pro-Choice claim that there should be no conditions whatsoever on that right, such as the viability of a fetus outside the womb, also compromises their position.

As we know, moral decisions are seldom completely clear or correct. Abortion involves complex moral/spiritual issues about whether a human life begins at conception or *when;* about how to weigh the value of a mother's actual life with a baby's potential life; about whether life is just physical existence or more than that, and *what* more; about whether and when society is prepared not only to claim interest in the life of the unborn but to provide needed financial and social support for the baby and the biological or adoptive parent or parents. Tough questions.

Q: Given all that, which position do you think is more morally compelling, Pro-Life or Pro-Choice?

A: Well, I'm Pro-Choice for several reasons. I've never known a woman who had an abortion who did not agonize over the decision and go ahead with it for any but urgent and compelling reasons, the most frequent being their inability to give a baby any kind of decent chance at life. To force women, regardless of circumstances, either to have the child, or risk a back-alley abortion, is dehumanizing them and demeaning their decision.

I don't believe people can credibly argue for the value of human life while at the same time supporting the death penalty and demeaning women by capping their freedom and questioning their ability to make weighty decisions, take responsibility and perform at the highest level in every area of life. I am outraged that some people who are against all abortion are also opposed to Planned Parenthood; sex education in schools; dissemination of condoms, birth control pills (or even information); or financial aid to poor people here or in Third World countries if there are any birth control measures attached. What does that say about women, or family values? I think that is unjust and immoral.

I think medically safe abortion should be available but increasingly rare. And I believe the way to do that is to emphasize and make accessible birth control aids and information for all people of child-bearing age. That's where the discussion and debate should go from here. God be with us as it does.

Q: Do you actually believe that reconciliation is possible between groups as entrenched in their positions as Pro-Choice and Pro-Life, or other groups like them? How can liberals talk with neo-cons? You think people in camps like that can be in dialogue? Or even should be?

A: What's the option to dialogue, really? There's a difference between talking and reconciling. To keep talking doesn't necessarily lead to reconciling, but it improves the odds. It does take courage to stay in dialogue, but it's cowardly to pull out because it's hard. Sulking isn't moral; it's indulgent. Talking is almost always possible.

But, as I said, reconciliation isn't always possible. The price can be too high and other values more compelling. But we can still hold our moral ground and seek creative options while we do. I think stressing birth control as the way to greatly reduce abortions is such an option for Pro-Choice. A big majority of people might well be for that emphasis, and that could turn down the public heat on the issue of abortion. I believe there are such options for many entrenched positions.

We have to ask those with views that are irreconcilable with ours how they see the gospel as supporting their view, and we have to tell them why we think the gospel supports our view. We need to ask if discrimination is a Christian, or American, value. Are we safer, say, from terrorism, if we do things that create more terrorists, not fewer; fewer friends, not more? Is promoting the hypocrisy of gay kids lying to families who would disown them for being gay a Christian value? Or supporting the hypocrisy of someone pretending to be straight when they're not? Or, in terms of family values, are we going to retreat into silence with our families and friends to preserve the illusion of caring and peace rather than trying to build trust by saying what we mean and meaning what we say? Or in support of family values, are we going to talk publicly about public policies such as health care, day care, and schools that are basic to keeping families together? That's the kind of talking we need because it can lead to dialogue and change and, if not reconciliation, at least improve its odds.

Just as the brave, brilliant women of the suffrage movement did, in getting women the vote in this country, we need to act and to raise our voices to express our faith views on critical, moral public issues without demonizing the other side or idealizing ourselves. God knows, that might eventually lead to honest reconciliation, rather than phony congeniality.

Q: Actually, I can't imagine anyone doing what you've been describing: opposing other people's position while keeping on talking to them about it.

A: Who is our best model for doing that?

Q: Jesus. Didn't work too well for him, did it?

A: That depends on what you mean by "work," doesn't it? Someone rightly said that Jesus preferred to be hated for who he was than loved for who he wasn't. That gives another meaning to what "works."

The point is not that things didn't work very well for Jesus, but that God wasn't defeated by what happened. We always need to be reminded to leave a little margin for God having something different in mind than we do. Often we assume that if we don't get our way, the whole ball game is lost. Most miracles happen slowly. Before the loaves and fishes could be discovered in the crowd, someone had to grind the grain, bake the bread, catch and clean the fish, walk however many miles to the gathering place, give up the loaves and fishes when asked. *Then* the miracle of feeding the five thousand happened. *Then* there were the twelve baskets of leftovers.

In our own way, we fish and grind and bake and walk and offer what we have, day by day. Most days, the only way I can get to mid-morning without figuratively having the wind knocked out of me, is to keep reminding myself that there is a lot more going on in this world than I can control, or need to. Then the question I need to answer is, if God was in Christ reconciling the world to himself, and if that Christlike God still goes on with that reconciling, how much am I willing to risk to be a part of that? *Part* of it, not the whole of it. When I answer that I want to be part of it, then the prayers stammer out, the courage rises, and the fun begins.

And now, it's time for us to take our leftovers home. Let's trust that wherever we go and however strange we may seem to be in this world, God will recognize us and, in some way, so will those who, meeting us, see us as their brothers and sisters. Go on boldly and in peace, beloved friends.

Sixth Sharing

It's been such a beautiful summer day, it's almost a shame to spend this evening indoors, but here we are together. I trust we're all grateful either for the time we've had together, or that it's almost over. In any case, let's gather with a prayer:

O God, you are in the beginning and end of all things, and in your sight a thousand years are like an evening gone. Still, you have assured us that not even one sparrow is forgotten in your sight. In our sight, then, that makes our evenings at least as precious to you as they are to us, and we even more precious to you than we are to ourselves and each other. In that assurance is our struggle to grow in awareness, trust, and love. And in that assurance is rooted our courage, peace, and hope for each day and night of our lives.

For the splendor of the setting sun, for the evening embrace of soft-lit mother earth, for the first awesome stars in the gathering darkness, for the glow in the eyes of each one gathering here, for the life of the One whose light no darkness can overcome, we are grateful beyond words enough to carry it to you, no matter how many trips they might make.

O gracious and holy One, be with us as we gather now, and as we scatter shortly, that the ways we go may be your ways. Deepen our gratitude into openness to new learning, our learning into courageous living, our living into accurate loving of you in each person we meet, each challenge we face, each gift we receive, each disappointment we endure, each sacrifice we make, each joy we experience, each breath that we draw, each chance that we take; through Jesus our Lord and brother. Amen.

Since this is our last gathering for a while, maybe some questions have been brewing and need to be asked now. Anyone?

Q: You've mentioned evil a few times without saying much about what it is. The word is used a lot politically, and most people use the word just to label enemies. What do you think evil is?

A: Evil is a terrible reality, not just a philosophical concept. It's something we experience. There doesn't seem to be another way to describe events such as 9/11, the Holocaust, and other episodes of genocide, slavery, the exploitation of women, the abuse of children, plagues—even Hiroshima—or natural disasters such as devastating floods, volcanic eruptions, earthquakes, all the horrific events in history. And yet, though the reality of evil is evident, it is nonetheless elusive. It's characterized primarily by how it kills, afflicts, or dehumanizes human beings. Yet the definition of evil is hard to pin down. When human beings unintentionally get in the way of natural events such as floods, earthquakes, or volcano eruptions, we may call the results "evil." But rather than calling them evil, it seems more accurate to call them tragedies, which at least partially result from the practice of building on flood plains or near volcanoes or over seismic faults, except with quake-proof structures. It would also be difficult to label as evil natural processes such as a lion hunting and killing a zebra—unless perhaps we were zebras.

Hannah Arendt, a philosopher who covered the trial of the Nazi Adolph Eichmann, wrote about the banality of evil. Her point was that evil doesn't apply to some special species of monsters. It applies to ordinary run-of-the-mill people like us. Its reality is commonplace. That's part of why evil is so elusive; it lurks where we don't think to look.

Take 9/11. It was a terrorist act with horrible consequences that probably qualify as evil. Is it possible to look behind that? Only with great effort! But still it seems morally and spiritually imperative to do so. Is it accurate morally to label Iraq, Iran, and North Korea as evil? The implication is that *all* the people of those nations are evil, or colluding in evil. Is that true? If it isn't true of *all* Iraqis, which ones is it not true of? How do we tell who is which?

Are Arabs, Muslims, or Saudis evil because twenty or so of them flew the planes into the Twin Towers and the Pentagon and crashed a plane in Pennsylvania that killed all the passengers? We're told that the terrorists were motivated by their religious beliefs. However misguided those beliefs were, and are, could the hatred they generated be rooted to some degree in any viable moral ground, or just complaint against our western culture and our history of dealing with their Muslim and Arab culture? Are there some unjust behaviors in which we collude that hatch their view of us as evil? If so, is there any way to responsibly address those complaints or alter those behaviors?

My point is that doubtless the *actions* that resulted in 9/11 were evil, but the *causes* of those actions may be more complex than the face they wear. Even when the reality of evil is evident, it is still elusive. This means that unless we take evil's complexity into account, our methods of dealing with it will frequently slip into becoming as evil as the evil we're trying to contain or eliminate.

Q: Are you saying that there's no answer to what evil is? Or is what you just said only part of the answer? I hope it's only part of the answer!

A: What I'm saying is far from THE answer. I don't think there is ever THE answer to the question, "What is evil?"

I think the primary feature of evil is that it intentionally causes pain, affliction, suffering, dehumanization, destruction, death. It diminishes, brutalizes, destroys life. Yet must evil always be done with unmixed intent? Can mixed intentions lead to acts of totally evil consequence? Add to those perplexing questions the reality that not all suffering and death is necessarily evil, nor as cruel or frightening as we may think. Sad, even tragic, are a truer face for them.

H. Richard Niebuhr said that God was not only the life-giver but the death-giver. In other words, God put limits on life. That means death can be seen as at least partly a gift. Of course, some deaths are tarred by evil, particularly "untimely deaths," such as those of children or young people or of soldiers in unjust wars; or deaths caused by cruel acts of murder, torture, abuse; or deaths of poor people around the world from curable diseases. The point is that simple definitions of evil slip away.

It is hard to say or see this, but some things we call "evil" are really not that but tragedies that result from the freedom that God wove into the whole created order. We know that freedom can be, and often is, misused or wrongly used by humans to terrible consequence.

But in addition to such misuse, any two free agents—humans and sharks, humans and viruses, humans and deranged cells, humans and flawed or mismatched genes, humans and other animals, and certainly humans with each other—can collide in ways that cause pain, loss, and death, such as birth defects and kids who suffer genetic diseases or are deformed by accidents, without those tragedies being the result of intentionality or human inclination. That tragedies are possible is the price of freedom, just as are joy and fulfillment. Freedom, which is the source of the capacity to love, can be frightening. That's why we're so quick to trade it for certainty and safety, or bow to those who promise them to us.

Q: But freedom doesn't account for all evil, does it? I mean, isn't there a difference between sin and evil? If sin is a misuse of freedom, is that what evil is as well?

A: I don't think sin and evil are the same thing. I'm not sure exactly what the difference is, and I do think they are linked, but I don't think they're the same. I'm struggling with that.

I think *intention* is involved in the difference. Sin is related to the subtle, or often not so subtle, intention of ME to be like God, or at least to be the center of everything, including

God's responsibilities and love. Sin certainly results in dire but often unintended consequences, hurting others through its self-preoccupation, blindness, and thoughtlessness. A distinction between sin and evil can get very confusing, particularly around events like 9/11.

On the other hand, I think evil is related to *nihilism*. Evil's intention is to deny that life has any meaning or value. Its intention is to deny God and destroy or invert life, along with all that nurtures life or gives it purpose. In a sense, while sin exaggerates the ME, evil tries to destroy the ME altogether. That's a bit simplistic, but that's the best I can do right now.

I think the worst kind of evil is moral or spiritual evil that makes life seem meaningless. Those feelings can overtake us when a loved one dies in a seemingly senseless way, or a child dies or is killed, or an exceptionally kind, generous person is raped, robbed, beaten. I think the tug of meaninglessness that we sometimes succumb to is why we are so addicted to the defenses of busy-ness and wealth, or consumption, or alcohol or sex, or the lure of comfort and certainty. It's our attempt to create meaning rather than accepting the meaning given by God and found through trust and compassion.

Elie Wiesel said that the most evil thing the Nazis did was to gas Jewish people enough to make them unconscious and then wake them up and tell them they had died and were eternally under the boot of the Nazis. Spiritual death, moral death, is the worst evil can inflict. That's what makes the images of hell or the threat of oblivion even more frightening than death itself.

I remember riding my bike as a teenager in my small South Dakota town, and a mean, drunk hobo stopped me, looked at me wild-eyed and said, "You gonna end up in hell, kid." That totally petrified me. Ending up in hell was more frightening to me than dying. The strict moralism of Midwest culture in that time made hell seem very real to a young boy. Plus, I got Ds in what the school called Deportment, so I felt particularly at risk. I never forgot that encounter, even though it seems irrational now.

Q: So where does evil come from? Do you believe there's a Devil, a Satanic being who generates evil and ensnares us in it? You know, as in the "Devil made me do it" line.

A: I think the image of the "Devil" is a way of personalizing evil but trying to keep it outside of ourselves. The Bible portrays the Devil, or Satan, as a fallen angel, or once-heavenly being who deceives, and tries to undermine the highest and best qualities of our being, as in the temptation of Jesus in the Gospels. The story of a "Devil" tempting Jesus may heighten the drama, but I believe the temptations were really the inward struggle of Jesus that continued on through his life. The Devil as a person may well have been a symbol of that life and death struggle in the same way Luke says Jesus sweat great drops of blood when he prayed in Gethsemane.[1]

I do not mean to restrict evil to a personal inward dimension but only to call attention to that dimension as a critical part of what evil involves. Evil is "in here" as well as "out there." That makes evil a very insidious, slippery operator who is in some sense as personal as we are but no more. I believe in that kind of Devil who, as Luther said, God could be rid of with a snap of the fingers, just as God could likewise be rid of us. Thank God for grace!

I think evil has to do with the Genesis story of the fall. The overreach and underreach of Adam and Eve, their rejection of their place in creation, which not only changed their status but disturbed the whole order of creation. They were free to make the choice to accept their place in creation or to try to elevate their place to a level with God or lower it to the snake-animal level. That choice is replicated over and over in the Bible, and in our lives, as is their effort to blame the serpent, making the serpent the embodiment of their own over/under reach.

The ability to discern good from evil was the twin of evil's birth. The sin of the human ME was the midwife of *actual* evil and the loss of innocence, but its twin, which is the ability to *discern* evil, is a gift from God.

---

1. *Luke 22:44*

That's the paradox of the story of the fall, I think. Adam and Eve sinned, but the resulting disordering of creation created a breach that was evil itself. A breach is a gap, a tear, an absence, a separation of what belongs together. In that sense evil is not so much *something* as it is *nothing*, emptiness, the void. *Nothing* is the opposite of God, who is in, with, and beyond everything. Evil destroys life by reducing it to meaninglessness of love, justice, hope, beauty, peace, and so to nothing. That's what frightens us about it.

Edward Albee's play *A Delicate Balance* is about a terrified married couple who appear at their neighbor's door and ask if they can stay with them. It turns out that what terrified them was "nothing." They were just sitting in their home and "nothing happened." That's close to what evil is. Spiritual nothingness leads to destruction of life. So we pray, "Deliver us from evil," which surely means not letting us be separated from God. So the prayer is, in its own way, answered in the praying of it.

Q: But you don't believe in the Devil, or the "evil one," as the newer versions of the Lord's Prayer have us asking to be delivered from?

A: I believe is that there is a kind of tempter that stalks us from within, that is part of us. So "lead us not into temptation" is linked to "deliver us from evil." In both Gospel stories (in Matthew and in Luke), it was the Spirit, or God, who led Jesus out into the wilderness where he was tempted by the Devil. The stories tell us that we need God if we are to deal with the temptation of ME-ism. We need to trust a Christlike God if we are going to resist other lesser gods, or give in to our lowest animal-like impulses. My belief is that Jesus' temptations in the wilderness weren't a once-and-for-all end of his wrestling with temptation, any more than it ever is for us. The paradox, the mystery is that to take God seriously means we will be constantly wrestling with everything that tempts us to take God less seriously than we take ourselves and God's image in us.

Martin Buber, the philosopher who influenced H. Richard Niebuhr, wrote of the "evil urge." As I read Buber, that urge is in us all. It was part of Jesus the man. So the deepest issue about evil becomes less the urge than what we do with it. The wilderness between urge and act is where wrestling with the tempter happens.

As destructive as evil is, I don't think it is irresistibly powerful. Buber said evil is never done with the whole heart, only good is. I believe that. I believe, along with the evil urge, there's good in us to be summoned and released, exercised. It's the good in us that generates our longing for God and stokes our capacity to seek and respond to God. That is what the process of salvation is about.

Q: What about demons? Do you believe in demons? They seem to be everywhere Jesus went. Now there are endless movies made about demons. What about them?

A: As with the Devil, I think there's something demonic in the world, and in us. Sometimes, some kind of sick spirit takes me over, and I lash out. I say hurtful things even when I know the hurt I'm inflicting. Then I sense what demonic is. Most of us have had that experience.

There's a wide range of the demonic, or "inner voices" as the root Greek word translates. That suggests the demonic could even extend to "voices" that tell people to commit crimes. Yet one of the striking things in the Gospels is that it was those considered possessed by demons who recognized who Jesus was. Were their voices angelic or demonic? It's hard to tell sometimes with some people we call crazy. I read somewhere that in medieval paintings the presence of holy persons wasn't signaled by a halo but by their being accompanied by demons.

What do you make of that? I know that my "demonic episodes" are quickly followed by a sense of my corruption, then contrition and prayers for forgiveness. There is some connection to my awareness of God in that reaction.

Q: But what does God have to do with evil? What does it mean to pray to be delivered from evil in the Lord's Prayer?

A: The simplest link people make between God and evil is the old statement, "If God is God, he is not good. If God is good, he is not God." The argument is that if God were almighty, then God wouldn't be good since God doesn't abolish evil. Or, if God is good and does nothing to abolish evil, then God isn't powerful and therefore wouldn't be God. But the argument is really a bait-and-switch trick, in my view.

In the first place, it doesn't allow that God could be almighty in many ways, not just in terms of power. Don't you suppose that God would not use his power to exempt us from the experience of evil because to do that would turn us into robots and the world into a precision machine with us as cogs? Or that God would use her power to bring out of evil events and experiences new choices for us to make in response? Or that we need to imagine more and different dimensions of what God's goodness is? Personally I suppose all that.

For example, suppose we keep repeating the mythic fall of Adam and Eve by our misuse of freedom, and that keeps unleashing evil to snarl up life and the world. In that case, God's goodness could be understood as not wiping us out but as staying with us to redeem us and the world. The oldest Christian creed says Jesus was "crucified, dead, and buried," then "descended into hell" before his resurrection. That points to God's goodness in pursuing us to the figurative depths of evil to save us. So rather than set goodness and almightiness in opposition, it would be more accurate to affirm God as a blend of traits who copes with anything.

Q: I want to ask a question about what's right with the world. I saw Robert Altman's film The Company, which is basically a documentary of the Joffrey Ballet. It was so moving, so beautiful, and I started thinking about the connection between beauty and our spiritual lives. How does the experience of beauty, and our ability to create something beautiful like that, connect to God?

A: Thank you! You've taken us in a whole different direction but into another area we can plumb but never get to the bottom of. Well, biting off more than we can chew is a lot better than chewing more than we bite off.

Let me start with how our ability to experience and create beauty connects us to God. My belief is that creativity is part of God's image in us. It was the early feminist theologians who went beyond calling God "The Creator" to calling God "Creativity." As long as creativity is taken to mean the ongoing activity of a personal God, and not just a human capacity or an abstract force, the insight of the feminist thinkers is very helpful and provocative. I believe we participate in God's creativity when we risk being creative in our lives and work. Creating beauty, or creating beautifully, is one dimension of creativity. It's like the dancers linking to the choreographer, as you suggested with your question.

Creativity is certainly evident in the arts and music and literature. But creativity is also part of product and treatment research and development, selling, legal work, business, political processes, diplomacy, home design, parenting, cooking. Creativity is part of almost every aspect of our lives—including how we relate to each other. Love is nothing if not creative. Justice is nothing if not creative. Peace is nothing if not creative. Or, to be exact, these are all dimensions of creativity realized in an ongoing way. A full life, a faithful life, is one of creativity.

There are a bunch of sister divinities named Muse in Greek mythology. The "Muse" came to mean the spirit of creativity we say we're waiting for when faced with an assignment to do anything creative. A visit from the Muse symbolizes the human experience of being swept up in a creative venture and sensing it involves more than our own effort, that it is a mutual activity with the spirit of creativity. I believe that's an experience of God. It's what those feminist theologians were affirming.

Q: But what if you're pretty dull in the area of creativity but are deeply moved by the creativity of others? Isn't that sort of a second-hand experience of the kind you're talking about?

A: Second-hand? I don't think so. I think being moved by an experience of beauty, appreciating it, is participating in the creativity. It's certainly not being *outside* of the experience. I once saw a poster that said, "Great poets need a great audience." I like the word "need" because a poem, like other creative things, needs to connect with someone else to carry on the creativity. Creativity is basically dialogical, a creative exchange between persons through whatever medium is involved.

I remember reading *Gift from the Sea* by Anne Morrow Lindbergh in which she writes about the primeval rhythms of the sea washing over her and drowning out hectic, routine rhythms and leaving her open to elemental, awesome, even eternal gifts of eternal treasures. In some way, that's what the experience of beauty is for us, though beauty seems too tame a word for it. It *is* too tame if we limit our view of beauty, and our experience of it, to its more familiar and repetitive expressions. Beauty is a mix of dynamic elements, as challenging as it is reassuring. It runs up and down the spine, shivering the soul in cadences of the kingdom.

Q: Can we go back to the question about what's right with the world? Can you name some things you would say are "right"?

A: I think what is fundamentally *right* with the world is that we live on a simply gorgeous planet. We take so much for granted when it comes to natural beauty! Today I went to the arboretum, and I felt like Moses encountering the burning bush, though it was too cold to take off my shoes. The sense of the holy was so strong. I often get that feeling in unexpected places, too, while walking city streets, or watching trees sway in a storm, or listening to a mockingbird sing at midnight. There's so much natural and humanly created beauty that mostly we take it for granted. There is an awesome beauty in storms and deserts, in faces of Down's syndrome kids, in wise old people and homeless beggars. Beauty spawns gratitude, and gratitude fuels moral responses, like caring for the environment and human family. Such responses are also what's right with the world. But our capacity to be awed is shrinking, so what's *right* with the world is often overlooked.

Another thing that is right is the self-corrective drive or urge that exists in people, and in nature. In 1980 I was visiting my parents in Portland, Oregon, just after Mount St. Helen's in Washington blew up. The whole top of that mountain came off. For weeks you could see the plume of smoke and ashes still spewing out. In a much shorter time than anyone predicted, however, Mount St. Helens began to repair itself. Green shoots pushed up through the ashes and lava. Animals began moving back in. Mount St. Helens is still missing its top, but it is close to being completely healed in the short period of twenty-five years.

The human body has that same capacity to heal from injury. So does the human psyche. Damage may leave scars, but healing is miraculous, really. We just help it along.

There's also an impulse in us to try to repair frayed, betrayed, and broken relationships. I would even say there is something in us that *needs* to do that. We want peace, we want justice. Most of us want to do, and often do, something to make things better for our families and children, as well as all the families and children around the world.

Loren Eiseley said that human beings have children who are dependent on them for a much longer time than any other species, and that there would be no human species if there weren't love that expressed itself in lengthy care of the young. It isn't just the urge of our DNA; it's something more. We seem to know that when children cry, the universe cries, and God cries. And when children laugh, the universe laughs, and God laughs. And that's something *right* with the world, isn't it?

Q: At the same time, there are all kinds of child abuse and exploitation and injustice and rampant consumption, ugly stuff like that. Don't they override the things that are right and beautiful?

A: I suppose on some bad days we might feel the ugly overrides the beautiful, but only briefly, right? I saw a cartoon in the *Philadelphia Inquirer* a few days ago. It showed a woman glued to her TV, saying, "It's just so horrible about Laci Peterson and her baby." Those murders *were* horrible, and the trial was as addicting for millions as a soap opera. But here's the needle in our haystack of all that's wrong: In the background of that cartoon were Sudanese mothers and their starving children. The cartoonist drew it, the newspaper ran it . . . and we got it.

We got the connection, and a lot of us have been moved to do something about that larger tragedy, and that what's *right* with the world: We have the Good Samaritan compassion to pick up the victims. It's right when we give to Dafur relief and call for our government to do something about the genocide. Sometimes we let a lot of things interfere with that impulse, but it's there.

Q: Loren Eiseley was a scientist, right?

A: Yes, an anthropologist with the gifts of a poet.

Q: Do you think scientists would agree with what he said about love and the care of children? Wouldn't most of them chalk it up to survival instincts, biological motivations? For me, the issue isn't just how God is connected to creativity and the arts, but to science and what science is about. What about that?

A: I doubt if there's a single answer all scientists would give to your question. I guess some would come down on the side of biology, some on the side of mystery, some on the side of love as a super-biological phenomenon. Then there's what the women and men who are professional scientists would say about it personally, as human beings.

But mechanical physicists who traffic in dense mathematical formulas in their explorations of the mysteries of the universe also describe scientific truths with terms such as elegance, harmonics, and beauty. I'm over my head here, but I take that to mean that aesthetics, beauty writ large, is as much a part of understanding the universe as quantum physics is. Creation is not only matter and motion, it is moral and beautiful. The relationships between its dimensions are graceful, symphonic.

Actually, a better metaphor for the link between creation and beauty is jazz (which is not always considered beautiful unless you expand the scope of that word). Jazz is about improvisation, different players interacting with each other extemporaneously, each responding to the unfolding music and rhythms being played or sung by others. Within the basic framework, jazz musicians create new and different chords and rhythms as they go. The same happens in the universe, in life, and in this world.

I would say God is the greatest improviser of all because God can make something like music out of anything—including disasters and death. All the unique but finite parts are improvised into the infinite whole, with things being changed but not lost in the process. That's why creativity is an accurate, if awkward, way to point to the dynamism of creation and God. Physicists might tear their hair out at my description, but never mind. I believe creation is spiritual as well as physical, though both terms are inadequate to capture the reality and the mystery of the universe.

So our little, improvising creativity partakes of the great improvising creativity of God. We find ways to do things a little differently from time to time, year to year, generation to generation, in everything from art to music to lawn mowing to figuring out how to help our neighbor. In that, I think we express a resonance with God.

Q: But science is about verification of theories by empirical tests and data, or at least mathematical proofs. How does what you're talking about fit that category?

A: What I'm talking about doesn't because it can't be quantified or verified by repeatable experiments. Actual life, as compared to clinical life, can't be stopped and rewound. The particularities and similarities of historical connections can't be repeated exactly either. So truth isn't limited to what can be verified by scientific method. The truths of life itself are comprised of unrepeatable incidents and events, and the Christian faith focuses on the particularities of individual uniqueness, as well as the particularities and similarities of historical connenctions that can't be exactly repeated either.

And yet, in another way, what I'm talking about is that there's an experimental element to the Christian faith. Jesus did new things that went beyond accepted practice and orthodox truth. He taught that there is truth that becomes compelling through living it, risking it. Truth emerges from life rather than being imposed on it. Jesus was always saying or doing things that involved a let's-try-this-and-see-what-happens attitude. Like being peacemakers, for example, or going the second mile, or caring for the poor, or healing a blind man by putting mud on his eyes, or calling Lazarus from the grave, or praying to "our Father." I think being fully human meant Jesus wasn't always sure what would happen when he said and did things.

Q: What you're suggesting is intriguing. But there has to be more to it to have a real impact, don't you think?

A: Do you know the Theory of Emergence? I've read about it, and I'm not very knowledgeable, but as I understand it the Theory of Emergence is a link between religion and science, or theologians and scientists who are beginning to have some conversations about it.

In essence the Theory of Emergence is that there is an impulse toward increasing or emerging complexity in the universe. Things move from simpler life forms to more complex life forms, and then those complex life forms become even more complex. Ultimately, consciousness emerges, primarily in human beings. That's followed by moral consciousness—and I'd add spiritual or God consciousness.

Then what emerges is the awareness that God has created us to be partners in this emergence process, not equal co-partners but asymmetrical junior partners. We have contributions to make to the emergence of what is to be. That seems to me to suggest that science has reintroduced God into the universe and initiated new ways for us to understand both the how and why of God's involvement in life. I'd say the Theory of Emergence is a scientific version of the creation in Genesis, rewritten with essentially the same evolving characters and plot. In a way, mystery is the common ground for both views, and neither view can, or needs to, rule out the other.

The Theory of Emergence is an exciting notion, and if I've construed it at all accurately, it's consistent with our experience that things get more complicated every year, decade, or generation. I have to call one of my grandkids over to help me figure out how my computer works, and they know exactly how to help me. I guess I'm more glad than apologetic about that because it seems to confirm that life becoming more complicated reflects God's creativity, as well as the process of science.

Emerging complexity reminds us that simple answers need to be reworked or rephrased in response to deeper, more wondrous possibilities, not just in the arena of technology, but also in the area of morality and human relationship. To be grasped by that is to be on a faith pilgrimage with Christlike creativity working in our lives and world toward the peaceable kingdom, a human community of justice and joy, and a healed and honored earth. Who knows how that will all come out exactly, but I find the mutual adventure what's *right* with the world.

Q: You make emergence sound inevitably good. What about the glitches that seem to accompany increasing complexity? What about the possibility of virtual, special effects movie weapons systems becoming real? Stuff like that.

A: Right. There is nothing inevitable about anything we human beings are part of, either good or bad. But I do believe God's purposes will prevail because, though God doesn't cause everything to happen exactly as it does, nothing can happen that God can't cope with à la the resurrection. For me, that's what it means to be a Christian and to follow Jesus. Dealing with glitches and threats is at least part of our responsibility as asymmetrical junior partners with God in the process of emergence, especially the emergence of moral and spiritual consciousness. By God's grace, tragedies and triumphs are not just about memorials and monuments but more: They're about a dynamic process of emerging possibilities.

That's part of what a resurrection is. It invites us to trust that our little efforts get taken up into a bigger picture. It gives meaning to what we are and do, meaning that is not just given by our loaves and fishes but which, by God's grace, emerges in the process we enter through faith and creative compassion, meaning that *finds us* as we move and rejoice into our lives as persons and as a society.

Q: Don't you think God has a plan for each of our lives? And that God's plan is what emergence is about, that things unfold according to God's plan?

A: As I have said before, I don't think God plans everything or controls everything. That doesn't make sense of love, of justice, of genuine growth, of mercy. What would mercy mean if God planned for us to commit the sin? Instead, I believe God *deals* with whatever happens without *causing* it to happen.

That's why I find the Theory of Emergence so intriguing. The future is open, not determined. It's more like the "Schrodinger's cat" analogy that Timothy Ferris used in *The Whole*

Shebang to illustrate indeterminancy. The gist is that, until we open the box, we don't know if the cat is alive or dead. Until then, it's potentially either one. The Theory of Emergence is that the future isn't known, or real, until we move into it and help shape its possibilities.

What I'm saying is that out of things that seem desperately wrong, redemptive possibilities emerge. Take cancer or disease from which progress toward cures and treatment emerges. That is our participation with God in the process. It's our way of joining in the improvisation that God is playing in the world and across the universe.

Or take another illustration. I just read that when a mother gives birth, she retains in her body what geneticists think are her baby's stem cells, and those cells remain in the mother's body as long as she lives. Apparently the purpose of those cells is connected to healing the mother's organs, if that's needed. Somehow God or nature is invested in keeping mothers healthy.

But the possibility that emerges from this discovery has to do with stem cell research and all the possible cures it might produce. If those cells in the mother *are* stem cells, and if scientists can find a way to get stem cells from women without going through an embryo, then we've got a whole different way of going at research with stem cells. If not that, then possibly with placentas. I think emerging possibilities like this are clues about how God and the universe work.

Now, I've been in over my head for quite a while. So we need to head for shore before I drown in this sea of science and religion I've gotten myself into.

Q: What does it mean to be faithful to God? I know what it means to me to be faithful to myself, to my ethics. I know what it means to be faithful in a relationship or a friendship. I think there are clues in those about how to be faithful to God. And you've given some clues in what you've said already. But how do we know when we're being faithful to God?

A: Some of the answer is in what you said—about being faithful to yourself and to friends. The first thing I'd say about knowing when we're being faithful to God is that it's dangerous when the answer is too clear and certain, when we *absolutely* know what God wants us to do, when we don't have any questions or reservations about it and don't need to check it out with anybody who would ask us tough questions about it. I think this kind of dogmatic certainty is very dangerous and the world has an abundance of people afflicted with it.

Then I'd say we need to keep praying about being faithful. Even Jesus had to pray all the time about how to shape his faithfulness to God. So I think there's always an uncertainty about whether we're being faithful to God.

But more importantly, we have a tendency to separate God from all the rest of life, as though somehow we don't get clues to what God wants from *all* the influences and information and experiences and people in our lives. I think all those are ways God comes to us and calls us. I believe a call directly from God is probably very rare. I don't doubt there are people who get such direct calls, but the test of such a call's authenticity is whether there is a blend of integrity and sacrifice and compassion in the person's response to it.

Here's a "for instance": choosing your life work. I've always chaffed under the assumption that ministers have a special call that's different from the call to be a teacher, lawyer, doctor, carpenter, or whatever. A career is about *what* we choose to do; a call is about *why* we choose to do it, no matter who we are or what the choice. A career choice is a process of discerning and responding to what excites or interests us, to what gifts and aptitudes we have.

A call is about honestly sorting out why we make that choice by discerning what we most deeply need to do for the integrity of our self, our relationships, our values, our hope to contribute something to others' lives, while reasonably supporting ourselves and our families. That's not a one-time decision or call; it's a continual process of discernment. A call is not just about our work, but how we do it, where, and what it means to our life. I think a lot of voices or influences are part of that discernment, not just the prevailing voice of our society. Since responding to a call is a large measure of what it means to be faithful to God, one of the important "voices" is prayer. If our decisions are all about ME and MINE, we'd better listen again to different voices—including our own truest one.

Q: Do you think a person can decide for himself or herself whether they're being faithful to God? Or do you think other people, or society, are needed? I'd say those are pretty unreliable sources.

A: I don't think other people, or society, should decide if a person is being faithful to God. What I do think is that the effort to be faithful involves a mixture of thought, imagination, emotions, listening, and prayer.

But that mix is partly shaped by parents, family, teachers, and friends. Some of those are trustworthy people who, along with others we trust, can help us check out our thoughts about what faithfulness to God means and how it applies to certain situations. They can hold us accountable for how our decisions and actions match. Faithfulness to God is not a totally solitary process; we need that support and accountability. We are nurtured by worshiping and praying and studying and working with others. Their compassion and energy and integrity are useful as a compass to direct us in being faithful to the God we see in Jesus.

Q: Suppose a church, like churches before the Civil Rights Movement, was preaching or practicing prejudice in the name of faith. I know even now there are lots of other examples. Doesn't it take individuals to stand against that sort of perversion? People like Rosa Parks, for example? Or even Jesus?

A: You make a good point. A church can be part of our faithfulness but not its final judge, as the Reformation taught us and we sadly relearn from time to time, ours being one of them. Lots of truth begins with individuals who are labeled heretics at first. There is definitely a strong prophetic element in the Christian faith. Prophetic voices or witnesses come from people trying to be faithful to God, and they always seem to gather others around them quickly, rather than just carrying on alone. Rosa Parks was a catalyst for the Montgomery Bus Boycott that gave momentum to the Civil Rights Movement. Jesus gathered disciples and left them as his legacy to the world after his resurrection.

Q: Those things seem so big and formidable. Is that what it takes to be faithful? That sets the bar pretty high, doesn't it? Reminds me of the old hymn we sang in Sunday school, "'Are Ye Able' said the Master, 'to be crucified with me?'" That was scary stuff to me then, and probably still is.

A: It was scary stuff to the first disciples, too. After the Last Supper, Jesus told them that they would all desert him, but Peter insisted he never would. That was bravado, not bravery, on Peter's part! All it took was a bonfire and three rumor mongers to make him fold. There's always a lot more bravado than bravery around. It's harder to be faithful than most of us would like it to be. We'd like to be people born on third base who go through life thinking they hit a triple.

There is a cost to the joy of discipleship. Faithfulness to God isn't all about success, security, and comfort. It's about risk and sacrifice and love with its sleeves rolled up to do justice and make peace. We know that, but as Thoreau said, the longest trip anyone makes is from the head to the heart. Being faithful is about making that trip, getting what we *know* down into what we *feel* and *do*. I'd also add that the round trip is just as long from the heart to the head, from convictions and feelings into imaginative thinking.

At the same time, I don't think faithfulness is always about *big* things, or being dramatically heroic, though it depends on your definition of heroic. I think we're faithful when we try to help our kids grow up right or when we work things out with spouses, partners, friends, enemies, going the second mile with them. We're faithful when we ask neighbors hard questions about peace and justice, and work with them toward those things where we live. Fidelity is about the way we live every day.

That's why it doesn't make sense to me for anyone to claim to have a private relationship with God apart from their relationships with other people. That's not Jesus' way. He shows that the next person we meet is the one we're called upon to relate to and love, the next situation is where we're "to do justly." When he told us, "In everything do to others as you would have them do to you; for this is the law and the prophets,"[2] Jesus didn't include a list of exceptions, such as hypocritical power brokers, poor people, prostitutes, repressive Romans, scorned Samaritans, frustrating enemies, hated tax collectors, disgusting lepers, or anyone else. That's why we call it the "Golden Rule," not the "Elastic Rule."

So the question is, "How do we treat other people, without exceptions, in a way that validates them, as well as God's image in us? Can we really treat them according to the Golden Rule?" Absolutely, it's very hard to do that! But just as absolutely, it's worth trying to do that as little else is. You see, ultimately it isn't so much about being crucified as it is about living abundantly and with spiritual integrity in the light Jesus casts on the way. It has to do with giving whatever loaves and fishes we have and asking God to multiply them for others. Just a little of the bread and fish of God's grace and mercy is all we need at the beginning, middle, and end of the day.

Q: We hear about what God will do for us if we just pray for it. Does what you say about the Emergence Theory mean we are to just be open to things as they come and trust that God is present through whatever happens? What does that imply for "asking" prayers? Are there things we shouldn't pray for if we trust God? Or that God can't do for us if we ask?

2. *Matthew 7:12*

A: I believe that prayer and whatever the Theory of Emergence might tell us about the universe are certainly not mutually exclusive. If we are in some way junior partners of God in shaping the emerging complexity of life, then I think all prayer is an essential part of that process.

Prayer is not only an expression of our relationship with God, it's a teacher of it. When any of us pray, we are addressing One who is in a different dimension than we are. I keep reminding myself of what God spoke to Isaiah: ". . . my ways [are] higher than your ways and my thoughts than your thoughts."[3] So who's to say for sure the what and how of God's answers to prayer? I think of C. S. Lewis saying that he prayed not to change God but to change himself. I know that happens to me and is one answer to prayer. And I know we can ask anything of God.

I just read an article in *The New Yorker* by Roger Angell, the guy who writes a lot about baseball. Angell's in his eighties now, and he went to a hospital to visit a friend he'd known most of his life and roomed with in college. The friend didn't recognize him. Angell was devastated that this man he loved was lost from him and was going to die. He went out and walked the streets in tears. He said "I felt again like a child who was crying for his mother to hold him."

Angell expressed a deep human need for God to hold us like a Mother. As limited, vulnerable human beings, we need to be held, and to pray for that. And just as it is our nature to ask to be held, it seems to be God's nature to hold us. Surely we're not too proud to ask like children. Isn't that part of what Jesus meant when he said, ". . . whoever does not receive the kingdom of God as a little child will never enter it"?[4] I know I often pray for God to hold me like a mother. I think God was present as a mother to Jesus on the cross because Mary stayed with her son while the disciples skittered away.

But it's important to understand that cuddling is not the same as coddling, and too many people seem confused about that. God doesn't coddle, but God does cuddle, hold, comfort, give peace. That's the human experience over the ages. We

3. *Isaiah 55:9*
4. *Mark 10:15*

pray uncensored from our heart and out of our need, then necessarily leave the answers to God. And I think our asking prayers also move us to hold each other.

Q: I've never heard of prayer being a teacher. Can you say more about that and how it relates to what you just talked about?

A: Part of what I mean by prayer "being a teacher" is that when I pray for God to hold me, it begins to dawn on me that what I'm really asking is for God to be with me so I won't be so afraid. I'm asking for courage enough to face the bad things, scary injuries, diseases, losses; for trust enough to accept my death with grace. I'm asking to grow in patience and wisdom and hope and love. I'm asking to be more concerned about my family and friends than about myself.

I believe, incrementally, millimeter by millimeter, I get a little less frightened as I pray. That's because prayer teaches us, and that itself is one way God answers our prayers. God's answer can be in our praying—there's a mystery for you! So I don't think there is anything out of bounds in prayer any more than there are any dumb questions for a good teacher.

Jesus called God, "Father," and that means God isn't an abstract force or an oblong blur, but a personal being whom we can trust as being at least as conscious, intelligent, wise, good, and compassionate as we are. *At least!* Surely consciousness and compassion didn't emerge from a blind, indifferent universe. I believe the Second Law of Thermodynamics says something like that.

Q: If we really believe there is life after death, then why are we afraid of dying? Okay, there's something unknown about it, but if we have faith, isn't what we call death just a period of transition? Can't we celebrate that when a person dies?

A: I resist calling a funeral a celebration of somebody's life. It's not that a funeral can't, or shouldn't, celebrate somebody's life.

It should, and does. But we've also lost, for a while, the one we celebrate, so a funeral or memorial service is also a ritual to help express our grief in that loss, not repress it. It is a way for people to express and pray for those whose grief runs deepest.

We sometimes sentimentally trivialize death as a way of avoiding it, but I don't think we should trivialize something that causes so much grief and sense of loss. Death is a tough reality, and it is scary. Only a fool thinks otherwise. Jesus didn't take death lightly. He didn't say, "Oh, boy, I can't wait!" Paul did, but Paul wasn't exactly a master of understatement. I believe that if we trivialize death, we don't learn from it. And I believe God *does* intend us to learn from death.

Last night I attended the wedding of Josh and Rebecca. I've known Josh since he was born, and his family even longer. I sat there thinking about the bride losing her sister, Sarah, to cancer just a couple of years ago. Sarah was a beautiful, spiritual person, a gifted poet who was only twenty-two years old. And there were Sarah's and Rebecca's mother and father watching Rebecca getting married and, at the same time, feeling the loss of Sarah. How could we say to them, "You should be celebrating, not feeling any sadness for Sarah." That would be cheap. It would be not respecting their loss.

Then it occurred to me that in all the major things in life—and even in the minor things—we are always stepping into mystery. We may get married, be madly in love, but we don't know how it's going to turn out. It's not all laid out. We can read books on something like *Twelve Steps to a Happy Marriage*, but the reality of marriage doesn't fit the page. The same is true if we stay single, or get a divorce, or lose a spouse, or have a career, or get fired or retired. We're *always* stepping into mystery.

We may have a child, and it's a joyful thing for the most part—except perhaps the part of waking and feeding her in the middle of the night, and all the fretting and fumbling we do as parents. Still, it's a joyful thing to have a child. This little life is a kind of miraculous gift. But sooner rather than later, we realize we don't have many clues about how this is all going to turn out. We don't know who this little person is going to become. We don't know what's going to happen to her. This little life is, and will remain, mostly a mystery all the way through. We do the best we can as parents, but we don't know. We do good things, and we make mistakes. By becoming parents, we step into the mystery of parenthood and childhood and humanity, the mystery of life and of death. Dying is another step into mystery. I think if we say too much about death one way or another, we are transgressing our limitations and missing its lessons.

Q: But we have to say something about it, don't we? I mean, as Christians? Doesn't faith have anything to say about death? What do you mean that we have something to learn from death?

A: Death teaches us how precious life is and how fragile. It teaches us to hold life gently, share it generously, care for it responsibly, live it deeply, be grateful for it daily. It teaches us that we're mortal—and all that "mortal" means. It teaches us humility. It teaches us that there is much we don't know but can find out, but also that there is much we can never know because we're limited creatures.

And what the gospel says, what faith says, is that death is in God's hands, and God deals with it. Death helps teach us to trust that God is going to deal with our death because, finally, we cannot, and we need God's help with it. I don't know what that means in any definite way, but to trust God makes me a little less afraid. Maybe by the time I'm ninety, if I live that long, I'll be a lot less afraid. Maybe I'll be even be glad when death comes if I've been drooling all over myself and being a general shambles. But I'll bet death will still have something to teach me.

Maybe the best that death teaches us is to accept it—not to surrender to it, but to accept it as part of who and what we are. W. H. Auden said something that I hold in my heart: "And Life is the destiny you are bound to refuse until you have consented to die."[5]

5. *W. H. Auden,* For the Time Being.

I believe that's true. Life and death are connected. To consent to our own death frees us to take the risks of life. Death teaches us that neither it, nor life, is trivial. We need to live in ways that protect people from premature death, those whose lives get snuffed out through violence or our casual indifference, or lack of food, potable water, and medical care. For us personally, we need to face into death and try to face it down—or *faith* it down—whenever the fear of it makes us cowards and rigor mortis sets in long before our last breath.

One last thing to learn from death: It is in God's hands, and if God has only silence or the abyss in mind, then praise God from whom all blessings flow. I don't believe that's what God has in mind, but neither do I think we can dismiss the mystery of death. To either trivialize it or sugarcoat it misses the mark. The mark is the cross, the empty tomb, the mystery, deep prayer—and God.

Q: Right now I know several people with difficult health problems, including a couple of kids. I also have some potential health problems that scare me. I pray for health for me and the others. What do you think about such prayers? Do God's purposes include such things as my healing?

A: I think clearly God cares about healing, yours and everyone else's. Look at Jesus and his ongoing work of healing people. So, I think your prayers for healing are good, honest, and faithful prayers. I also think they are answered in some way by a God whose wisdom and love outrun our own.

So I imagine God's answers would probably outrun exactly what we want. And that's the key. We all know people who prayed for healing and didn't get what they hoped for, and thought it was because they lacked faith enough for God to grant it to them. I don't believe God plays with us that way. I think God's answer to those prayers can move in a different and unexpected direction. But I go back to what I said, namely, that the real issue is learning to be less afraid of being vulnerable to pain, suffering, and death. Less afraid, so we can give up some of our fearful grip on ourselves. Less afraid, so we can live and die in more peace, hope, and trust.

I also believe we need to be mindful, and heartful, of the difference between healing and curing. Healing refers, I think, to an inner peace and wholeness, an "underneath are the everlasting arms" assurance that is deeper than physical cures. I believe some prayers result in miraculous cures, but such cures are still temporary at best. They do not eliminate our mortality. Healing can involve a cure, but not necessarily. Healing refers to a deeper, more lasting state than a cure. I believe healing is a greater answer to prayer than a cure. Healing is something to pray for whether or not we have an illness or injury.

I recently read that sixty to ninety percent of visits to doctors are for stress that manifests itself in physical problems. There are increasing numbers of studies showing how the mind and body are connected that confirm the unity of mind, body, and spirit. They also show that prayer, meditation, slowing down, deep breathing, and yoga are all ways to promote healing.

The people Jesus healed came to him with their need. So can we. But if we become obsessed only with our own well-being, health, and security, that obsession can dehumanize us—and our group, economic class, gender, race, or nation. Fear for personal, group, and national security then crowds out concern for justice, for peace, for healing of the human family. And, like stress, that obsession contributes to, if not causes, an epidemic of sickness of our minds, our spirits, and our body politic. We can see something like that happening these days.

Q: So are you saying that praying for healing is good, but don't pray too much for it?

A: No, I'm not saying that at all. I don't think it's likely that we can pray too much about anything, including our own curing or healing or that of loved ones. I'm just saying that when the concern for our own healing, health, or security becomes an obsession, it becomes a mind cramp that can lead to stress that causes physical as well as public illness. I believe we should pray for healing, then follow the prayer into wider circles. Prayer teaches us about those wider circles, if we pay attention.

Let me tell you a story. One late December day we were racing home from the Outer Banks to beat a threatening blizzard, when my cell phone rang. It was my son David, sobbing as he told me that his seven-year-old daughter, Julya, had hit a tree while skiing and had severe head trauma. She'd been airlifted to a Pittsburgh hospital, and twice on the way she had to be coded to get her heart started again. She was in the pediatric intensive care unit. David was sobbing so hard he could hardly get the words out: "Dad, pray for Julya. Pray for us." David is an athlete, an attorney, strong, clear-headed. It would not be easy for him to ask anybody to pray for him. But he did: "Pray for us, Dad."

I started praying as hard as I could as we rocketed down the highway. I prayed for God to be in Julya's head to heal, to be in her lungs and her heart, to help her stay alive. I visualized God doing that. Then I began to think, why should God do that for my granddaughter and not for the other kids in pediatric intensive care with her, in that hospital, in every hospital, and all the sick and wounded kids around the world? That didn't stop me from praying for Julya, but it did start me praying for those other kids as well. And for Julya's parents and family, and for the families of all those other kids.

Prayer teaches us to pray for others as well as ourselves. It teaches us to pay attention. It teaches us compassion at a profound level. Prayer is forever leading us further and deeper toward others and God. I believe God answers prayers in a lot of different ways, through doctors, parents, other people, and in ways we never know about.

Q: Things turned out okay for Julya, right? Were your prayers part of that, do you think?

A: Yes, but I don't know exactly what part, or how big a part. Part of the answer to my praying is what it taught me. But there is a mystery to healing, to the way illness works and how it progresses, or doesn't. Even medical advances don't dispel the mystery.

You may remember my telling you that when my divorce was becoming unavoidable, I visited my parents in Oregon. My mom was far along in her Alzheimer's illness, and its course was relentless. Well, to finish that story, after arriving and talking with Dad a while, I started over to see Mom in the nursing facility. Dad said Mom wouldn't know me or understand what I was talking about. As I walked to her building, I prayed for her, and tears came to my eyes. It's hard to lose your mother twice.

When she first saw me she asked, "Does your other know you're here?" What a poignant, layered question that was. I started to talk with her, and she was pretty unresponsive. Then I said, "Mom, I'm going to get divorced."

For ten minutes my mother was there with me, clear as a bell, asking questions, making comments, as though she had nothing wrong with her. She was very perceptive, very accurate in her observations, sad about the divorce but supportive of me. I was amazed. Then she was gone again.

I don't know where she came back from for those awesome minutes, and I don't know where she went afterward. But somehow her soul, her mother core, was intact and responsive. Her brain was compromised, but not her heart and will. The mystery of those "eternal" minutes is branded on my soul.

How does God answer our prayers? I don't know. I only know strange things happen and God is sneaky. So I try to be watchful. Maybe prayer has nothing to do with those strange things . . . but maybe it does. I believe it does. Some studies show some evidence that it does. Scientists don't always agree with the evidence or the stringency of the studies, but it does seem that people who are prayed for have more rapid recoveries and do better in the hospital and do better with their illnesses than people who are not prayed for. Part of the mystery of it is that they not only do better when they *know* they're being prayed for, but they also do better even when they *don't* know they're being prayed for.

Q: Then what about Rebecca's sister, Sarah? She died even though everybody was praying for her—me, my family, my sister's whole church. I'm sure Rebecca prayed for Sarah all the time. When Sarah died, Rebecca felt, and still feels, betrayed by God. She says she's an agnostic.

A: In some way all of us are agnostic because I think doubt is faith in another form. Faith is not knowledge; questioning and belief are joined in our experience. It was amazing to me at the wedding when both Rebecca's father and mother said they knew Sarah was with them. Yet Rebecca had said her father was agnostic, and her mother probably, too. I believe there is integrity in their agnosticism, given their loss and its still-fresh pain.

I'm just saying that I believe the prayers offered for Sarah, Rebecca, and Josh, were answered in some way. Rebecca and Josh had a long talk with me a week before the wedding. They were very clear about what it means to be married, and very committed to the hard work of loving each other. They had gone through too much deep water with Sarah before she died for them to be naïve about love. I know the pain and grief is still there, but it's becoming more redeeming than debilitating for them. I believe prayer, in whatever searching way they do it now, is part of what makes it that way.

When we pray, we are affirming that there is someone there, listening, someone to whom we reach out almost instinctively and intuitively. That reaching in itself goes beyond all our words, which only stumble after the longing hardwired in us. Paul points at it when he says the Spirit intercedes for us "with sighs too deep for words."[6] Those sighs echo our sighs and stumbling words, which are the wager on God we make in our hearts. I believe it's worth the wager, and I make it every day.

6. *Romans 8:26*

Q: I've never heard anyone process things the way you do. You don't use words like omnipresence and omniscience and all that jargon. Did you have this kind of view from the beginning, I mean growing up in your family? Where did this way of thinking about and practicing faith come from?

A: I was a birthright Methodist in Nebraska and South Dakota, then in Oregon. But the truth is that I spent the first twenty-one years of my life in the locker room. Being a ball player was the most important thing in the world to me. I did well in school, but I didn't really think a lot about these things. In college I was a philosophy major, and I kept expecting that the next philosopher I read was going to tell me "what it's all about." I didn't actually understand half the guys very well anyway, but none of them turned my lights on. I'd get all bent out of shape about the epistemological dilemma or the ontological argument, and now I can't remember exactly what those were.

In a sense, going from philosophy, psychology, and history into theology was like coming in for a landing. Lots of theologians made an impression on me, especially my Yale professor H. Richard Niebuhr, who didn't teach us a theology so much as how to think theologically. And I was always drawn to the process theologians because they just made more sense to me. You can hear that in much of what I say. But the things that have been most shaping of my life have been the things that broke me, the first of which was an emotional, mental breakdown.

It happened over forty-five years ago. After I graduated from Yale Divinity School, I went on to graduate school to get a Ph.D., with the hope of becoming a college professor. I got a fellowship to do that, but I had to take a part-time church job to provide for my family. At that point, we had two kids, one almost three, the other almost one. After a year or so, the church needed a full-time minister, and I couldn't leave because then I'd have no way to take care of my family. The door of graduate school started to squeak shut. I stopped going to graduate school by deluding myself into thinking that the decision would be temporary. Then we had a third baby, and in two more years, a fourth. I didn't want to be a minister, but I felt trapped.

Without going into a long, drawn-out explanation of it all, I was terrified. Out of what seemed the blue, came my breakdown. The wheels came off of everything. I was shattered. I prayed, but to no avail. I was so down, suicide became a real possibility. I had to keep my breakdown a secret because in those days it was a stigma to have that kind of problem. No one, not even family, really knew what I was going through. I was ashamed, desperate, and praying frantically. No deliverance came, and any faith I had was circling the drain. My breakdown precipitated a dark night of the soul for me.

One night after midnight, alone in the living room with some pills and a bottle, I was about to commit suicide when my little four-year-old son came padding down the stairs from bed, got up on my lap, and went to sleep. He'd never come downstairs like that before. It ended my thoughts of suicide.

Then one Saturday a young doctor in the church, David, came to me and asked what was wrong. He could tell something was. I told him, and he offered to find me a psychiatrist and help pay for my treatment. The psychiatrist, John, was not only skilled, but a wonderful human being, a young guy who was open to sharing his own struggles with me so I didn't feel so wrong or guilty or alone in mine. The healing at the depths took a long time and is still going on. I pray it will be as long as I live.

My breakdown chewed up, spit out, and made me rework all my theological stuff. For that, I am grateful, though I hope never to go through that valley of the shadow again. It was a kind of death, and a kind of resurrection. I'd gotten to the point where I felt the demons had won, that I was nothing, and nobody gave a damn. Then came my little son in the middle of that night; then into my darkness came David and John. So looking back, I believe that's how God answered my prayers.

For anyone who wants quick answers, clichés, bumper-sticker thoughts about faith, I don't have them—not for myself, not for anyone else. That experience, my later divorce—and hearing my adult kids talk in family therapy after the divorce about the ways in which I had hurt them—have all influenced me profoundly and taken me deep down into my own life, my own being, into the mystery of God and grace. I've pretty much stayed there. I feel very humble, and I am very grateful.

I know things about myself that I assume are true at the core for other people as well. So I think and write and preach and talk and counsel, believing that maybe some people will hear and connect to it in a way that's helpful to them. That's all I have to give. And it's a gift to me.

Basically what I do and say, in this group and out, is my own way of trying to make my faith, and yours, have some integrity and some deep congruence with our real lives by helping us and others believe in God, by being more believable ourselves. When it's all said, but not yet done, our lives are our loaves and fishes to be blessed, to feed the hungry, and to be gathered up to keep going and growing in faith.

So as we close, let me repeat Martin Luther's theological summary comment: "Trust God and sin on boldly." I hope you understand more of what he meant. And don't forget the leftovers as you leave. The leftovers are soul food.

Other Books by Ted Loder

Guerrillas of Grace: Prayers for the Battle
136 pages, 0-8066-9054-2

For nearly two decades, this classic collection of tough, beautiful, and earthy prayers has lightened hearts and dared spirits to soar.

The Haunt of Grace: Responses to the Mystery of God's Presence
192 pages, 0-8066-9034-8

From the pen of one of today's most visionary spiritual thinkers comes a book of profound explorations on the mysteries and marvels of faith, love, and life. Believing that mystery is at the very heart of faith, Loder delves deep into the "sneaky" ways God surfaces in the muddle of everyday experience.

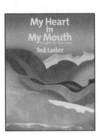

My Heart in My Mouth: Prayers for Our Lives
160 pages, 0-8066-9032-1

Loder's gutsy, grace-filled prayers break out of all formulas into heart-felt, mind-opening, soul-searching ways of reaching to God.

Available wherever books are sold.

Other Books by Ted Loder

Tracks in the Straw: Tales Spun from the Manger
176 pages, 0-8066-9014-3

In a memorable Christmas book full of surprises and wonder, Loder offers fifteen nativity stories and fables that bring forth an amazing set of characters, animals, and unexpected visitors who witness, in one way or another, the life-changing mystery of the nativity.

Wrestling the Light: Ache and Awe in the Human-Divine Struggle
190 pages, 0-8066-9039-9

Loder gives expression to the depths and joys of the human struggle in these intensely personal prayers, complimented by six powerful stories.

Available wherever books are sold.

About the Author

The Rev. Dr. Theodore W. Loder was the Senior Minister of one of Philadelphia's most unusual churches, the First United Methodist Church of Germantown (FUMCOG), for almost thirty-eight years. With imagination and intensity, Loder led FUMCOG to the forefront of artistic endeavors, political activism, and social justice. His congregation has been a Public Sanctuary Church, a founding church of the Covenant Against Apartheid in South Africa, a Reconciling Congregation that advocates for the rights of homosexual persons.

Loder's own social action grows out of a long history of involvement in social causes, including marching with Dr. Martin Luther King Jr. in the sixties. Loder is co-founder of Metropolitan Career Center (a job-training program for high school drop-outs); co-founder of Plowshares (a non-profit housing renovation corporation); and co-founder of Urban Resource Development Corporation (an ecumenical effort to rehabilitate abandoned houses). He has also served on the Philadelphia Mayor's Advisory Commission of Children and Families.

For many people who have "given up" on the church, Loder brings a breath of fresh air. His blend of scholarship (cum laude degree from Yale Divinity School, a university fellow of the Yale Graduate School, and two honorary doctorates) and creativity (named by the *National Observer* as "One of America's Outstanding Creative Preachers") stimulate his refreshing openness to hard questions, to change, to relevance, to justice, and to joy.

Dr. Loder currently serves on the National Advisory Board of the National Council of the Churches of Christ in the U.S.A.